No
Man
Walks Alone

No
Man
Walks Alone

Frank K. Ellis

LIEUTENANT COMMANDER, UNITED STATES NAVY

Fleming H. Revell Company
Westwood, New Jersey

PHOTOGRAPHS

Official U.S. Navy photographs; photographs by Bill Ray, *Life* Magazine © Time Inc.; photographs by Ernest Reshovsky, Pix; photograph reproduced by permission from the August, 1967, issue of *Good Housekeeping* Magazine, © 1967 by the Hearst Corporation.

This book is dedicated to my wife, Christine Cecile, who so courageously and faithfully has shared with me the challenge of life recorded herein, and to the four little lives that give a special purpose to this challenge—David Alan, Debra Ann, Dana Angela, and Daniel Andrew.

Contents

Contents

Introduction

FRANK ELLIS is five feet ten inches tall—or, if you happen to be from the National Aeronautics and Space Administration (NASA), he'll make it clear to you his height is adjustable from four feet eleven (without his plastic legs) to any required height. Just design the space capsule as the scientists think best, and Frank will adjust himself to fit into it. No problem at all.

New ideas and concepts—which turn his lack of natural legs into an advantage, or at least reduce the practical differences between a double-amputee and a normal man to near zero—are part of Frank Ellis' daily thinking. "I'll tell you one thing," he says. "They'll never have to worry about my toes getting frostbitten in a survival situation."

We interviewed Frank at his home in Monterey, California. Being a Navy man, Frank and his family move around a lot, so we were lucky to catch up with him in such a beautiful spot as Monterey. He picked us up at the airport in a well-used Chevrolet station wagon, and we confess it took a mile or two before we were convinced Frank could actually drive the car safely. Our first reaction to a double-amputee was like anybody else's . . . we were in the company of a "handicapped" man, and, of course, he wouldn't be able to function as well as a "normal" man. It is our opinion that Frank Ellis' consuming desire to become an astronaut, or to be returned to the unrestricted flight duty for which he is clearly qualified, stems equally from his personal wish to be of maximum value to the Navy and from his wish to prove to people—military men, medical men, and the general public, like us— that most opinions regarding the "handicapped" are incredibly outdated and useless. Frank is living proof that, except for a few minor functions, an amputee can be as capable in his job as the average highly trained Naval aviator *with* natural legs. The unrealistic concepts, both emotional and technical, with which the "handicapped" are regarded by others not only are a frustration to persons like Frank, but result in an unwarranted loss to the nation of capable, skilled men.

We hadn't yet thought about any of this when he pulled the station wagon into his driveway, but we did know he had a lovely blonde wife and four wonderful children. They were waiting for us with big healthy California smiles on their faces. In order of appearance that afternoon in June, 1967, they were: Chris (Frank's wife), David and Daniel (eight and four years old, respectively), Debra, seven, and Dana Angela, five. Chris offered us tea and cookies on the sun-drenched porch, and while we got our feet back under us after the cross-continental plane ride, we watched in growing astonishment as Frank did the following:

A. He happily gave in to his children's request to push them on a rope swing.

B. He walked down the porch steps, crossed the lawn, and, as nimbly as you please, scooted down a steep bank, forded a small stream, and clambered up an equally steep hill to the rope swing.

C. He gave his own children (and a few belonging to neighbors) several uproarious rides on the swing, then retraced his steps and proceeded to supply a push to another child who had climbed on a tire tied to a rope in the backyard.

D. He did all of this—pushing, pulling, climbing, descending—without missing a step or being noticeably out of breath, and we would defy many men of Frank's age (thirty-four) to duplicate it so gracefully.

It was easy after that performance to ignore the word "handicapped" in regard to Frank Ellis, and we got right down to the business of his book.

He told us bluntly that he would not be interested in writing anything that was sensational or exaggerated, and that his faith in God was simple and direct, not mystical or full of complicated drama. He would tell his story exactly as it happened, quoting from the records as much as possible; and if this were the kind of book we wanted, then he would do it for us. He hoped the book would help others, especially those who have suffered loss or considered themselves hopelessly handicapped, but he was not seeking personal publicity, nor would he accept editing that made a superhero-type out of him.

We couldn't have admired his attitude more, or agreed with him more heartily. We assigned an editor to work with Frank; and, a few weeks later, *No Man Walks Alone* began to be dictated into a tape recorder in his living room.

This books remains true to Frank's desire—it is straight and uncomplicated: an exciting, almost unbelievable narrative that needs no embellishment from the publishers. But we are going to take one liberty.

In the dark days of 1963, almost a year after Frank Ellis' Cougar jet had crashed, resulting in the loss of his legs, it seemed certain not only that he would never fly again for the Navy, but also that he would be retired from service. Among those who appealed to the Navy to continue Lieutenant Ellis on active duty was Commander W. T. Marshall, Jr., Ellis' commanding officer at the time of the accident and after his return to duty. He wrote:

> Lt. Ellis is beyond doubt the most courageous man I have ever had the pleasure to know.

As publishers of *No Man Walks Alone,* we exercise the right to include that deserved compliment in this book. And no one who reads more than two pages of Ellis' story will doubt for an instant why we have included it.

The Publishers

1

Holy Mackerel!

MANY PEOPLE have asked me what I was thinking about when I finally realized my jet fighter was going to crash, probably taking me with it because I was only sixty-five feet above the ground, which is about 235 feet too low for a successful, according-to-the-book, ejection.

Was I praying?

Or thinking of my wife and children?

Or was my life passing in fast review before my eyes?

No.

I remember I said one thing: "Holy mackerel!"

And I recall thinking of something else as the Cougar hurtled nose-down toward the ground at about 135 miles per hour: "I've made hard landings on a ship, but this one will be *really* hard!"

And so, in this matter-of-fact way, I closed the book on what, by any reasonable odds, should have been the last words and thoughts in my life.

All of this occurred on July 11, 1962. I'd picked up the F-9 Cougar in Norfolk, Virginia, and was ferrying it to Point Mugu Naval Air Station in California. I made fuel stops in Tennessee and New Mexico, and was on top of the world as I flew west toward California, admiring the scenery over the Painted Desert in Arizona.

I called Mugu tower for landing instructions as I passed over northwest Los Angeles, and then followed the coastline north toward the field, descending to 1,500 feet and reducing speed to about 300 miles per hour about six miles from touchdown. Everything was hunky-dory.

The first inkling of trouble came when I was at 1,000 feet in the landing pattern and traveling at 180 miles per hour. I could raise and lower the nose of the aircraft with my stick, but the elevator trim mechanism, a system designed to aid the pilot in the control of his aircraft's nose attitude, didn't respond.

I switched over to the "emergency" trim system, but it, too, was on a holiday. However, I still had plenty of stick control, so I elected to continue my approach. I turned the emergency system to "off," concentrating solely on stick control. I was now doing about 135 miles per hour at approximately 300 feet altitude. The runway was a little off to my left and I was turning into the runway heading when complete nose-down trim failure suddenly occurred—and then things started to happen, faster than I can write them here.

The nose drove full down. . . . "Holy mackerel!" . . . I tried vainly to pull the nose up with
my stick . . . grabbed for face curtain over my head
that would trigger the mechanism to eject me from
the plane . . . trailer park and trailer ahead of me,
in my flight path . . . forget about ejecting . . . pull
up gear and add power to increase speed and
maybe clear trailer . . . plane still sinking, but able
to alter heading with ailerons toward open fields . . .
"I've made hard landings on a ship, but this one
will be *really* hard!" . . . clear of trailer! . . . in-
stantly eject . . . huge fireball!

That's all I remember of the crash, though I've
been told I mentioned pains in my chest, back,
and left leg, and talked freely with the medical
personnel in the Navy ambulance en route to St.
John's Hospital in nearby Oxnard. I was definitely
in a state of shock, and I was delirious for three or
four days. It was later reported that one of the first
questions asked me when the crash crew arrived
was what had happened to me and my plane. I was
asked this question again on my way to the hospital, and neither time could I answer. An hour after
the crash, while lying in the hospital awaiting
surgery, I managed to ask what had happened to
me. When they asked me if I had ejected, my
strange answer is still in the records to see: "I
don't know if I was landing or taking off."

Navy investigators surveyed the crash scene, questioned eyewitnesses, and pieced together the full story as well as it can ever be known.

I had ejected from the aircraft at an altitude of about sixty-five feet, and had been hurtled through the fireball caused by the plane's crash, and then through the tops of several eucalyptus trees, which slowed my fall. My parachute had partially opened, slowing me down even more as I plummeted through the trees; and by the time I hit the ground, my speed had been considerably reduced.

I was alive—but barely. My right leg had been amputated below the knee, and I had compound fractures of the left leg. My back was broken, and so were several ribs. Needless to say, I had several cuts and burns. I must have been a beautiful sight.

I was in surgery for about three hours, then suffered a postoperative coma, and was loaded up with narcotics and other drugs. It wasn't until the fifth day after the accident that there was any hope of questioning me intensively, and even then it was carried on in one-hour sessions only. I think a full week passed before I realized I had lost a leg— the sheet sloped too much on the right side of the bed, and I peeked under for a look.

I've been asked numerous times what my reaction was at that moment. I can report truthfully that my only reaction was, "I'll be darned, it's gone!" I was the luckiest guy in the world just to be alive, and I knew it. A leg seemed a small price to pay for survival, and I had no doubt about *staying* alive, either.

I was removed from the critical list after my second week at St. John's, and was transferred to the United States Naval Hospital in San Diego, just a few minutes from our home in Coronado. On that flight from Oxnard to San Diego, Chris got her first hint of what was to come when I exclaimed from my wire stretcher lashed to the deck of the aircraft, "Gee, Honey, it seems good to fly again, even in this capacity!"

Two days later, Chris entered Coronado Hospital and added another member to our family— Dana Angela, eight pounds eight ounces. That then brought our family count to five, and three of us were in the hospital!

One unresolved problem in my situation continued to be my badly smashed left leg. Infection was increasing, causing considerable pain, fever, and loss of weight (I'd dropped from 160 pounds to under 100). At one point, the fever reached 105°F, and it was necessary to cut away part of my body cast so that towels soaked in ice water and alcohol could be placed on my stomach and chest. For some Spartan reason, I refused to take pain-relieving drugs, and although I could stand it during the day, the constant pain made sleeping almost impossible. I have strong memories of pounding my head on the mattress to put myself to sleep, and I recall one day in particular when I

19

had to tell Chris: "Don't talk to me or touch me, Honey. Just sit there." Finally, I couldn't even get to sleep anymore, and I welcomed the pain-killing medicine.

The Navy surgeons operated several times on my left leg, but on September 14, two months after the crash, the decision was made to amputate. Frankly, this final amputation was a relief, and within a week my condition had improved tremendously. Fever, pain, immobility, weight loss . . . everything decreased remarkably, and I even got back my critical taste for food. I was clearly on the road to recovery.

Essentially, this is the end of the "crash" portion of my story. During those days in the hospital, I never doubted for a moment that I would return to active duty and resume my career as a naval pilot. Apparently, all I talked about was flying, because after the final operation on my left leg, one doctor leaned over and said: "I hope this is your last operation. We're getting tired of hearing about airplanes everytime you're anesthetized."

This confident expectation of flying again was, as I learned later, a little naïve on my part. I was now a double-amputee, and I was to find out in the near future that, as far as the Navy was concerned, I was slated for swift retirement. Countless obstacles would have to be hurtled, high-level opinions would have to be changed, and many precedents would have to be set if I were to remain a naval aviator. I was starting from below the bottom of the barrel.

But at that time I didn't know it. I was alive and happy and supremely confident. I expressed my feelings in a letter to my friends: "I'm just quite delighted my rib and back injuries healed as they did, and that God spared my life for a reason or reasons that time may disclose."

With that thought firmly in mind, I started agitating for some artificial legs. It seemed to me that things were progressing too slowly in getting artificial limbs built for me. I had to make a first step toward resuming my naval career, and I had to have feet to do it on!

2

Early Years

I WAS BORN in Painesville, Ohio, July 26, 1933. My earliest memories are of Hudson, Ohio, where I lived until I was six, and I can recall many happy hours spent on the Western Reserve Academy Farm and the pleasant Christmases in Hudson during the snowy winter months. For the most part, these were carefree days in Hudson, marred only by the separation of Mother and Dad because of his serious drinking problem. Fortunately, Mother had a small private income, and the Ellis children—which included my older sister, Mary K., and my younger sister and brother, Connie and Jimmy—never lacked anything necessary to our health and comfort.

I was to see my father only infrequently during my childhood, including a hopeful but discouraging year or so when he and Mother reached a reconciliation that proved unsuccessful. This exposure to the effects of alcoholism has left an indelible impression on me. I don't drink today, and never have. One of the most saddening things I can think of is a teen-ager taking a drink to be sociable, to be one of the crowd. I'm impressed only with his weakness and the possible problems which may ensue.

My mother's health didn't prosper well after the separation, and her doctor advised her to move to a warmer climate. This was when I was in first grade, where I remember learning how to make jelly and to take care of white mice and ducks.

My *second* year in the first grade was spent in Clearwater, Florida—and this seemed more promising. At least I learned something more useful scholastically. Some of my classmates in Florida were going to school barefooted, but they could do a little reading and writing, and this was a considerable step upward from the jelly-making brigade.

I don't mean to imply that I was an outstanding student and just panting to go to school and learn my lessons. On the contrary, I was far more interested in playing marbles, swimming, building huts, etc., than in applying myself in school. There was something about that beautiful Florida sunshine and clear air that made school seem uninviting. We lived right on the beach, and you can imagine how hard it was to turn my back on all that magnificent water and sand and trudge off to school.

Third grade was a particularly memorable year —Cyril, a French friend I'd rounded up in school, and I were spanked in school almost daily by a teacher whom we almost frustrated to death. I recall an Easter-egg hunt that year which our class was holding down by Clearwater Bay. Cyril and I walked down there with the rest of the class dutifully; but when it came time for the children to return to school, Cyril and I hid in the bamboo and hitchhiked home across the causeway and back to the beach.

Well, the teacher was frantic. Two of her children were lost; and knowing our remarkable ability to get into every kind of mischief, she expected the worst. It turned out all right—I'll not go into the details of what happened after I got home and when we went back to school (you can guess)— but if that poor teacher is still alive today, she probably remembers Cyril and me better than any of the children she ever taught, or at least tried to teach.

My talent for getting less than the maximum learning out of school was carried over to Sunday school and church. In Clearwater, my family attended the big, pink Peace Memorial Presbyterian Church. I guess I spent most of my time there sitting in the balcony, counting the panes in the big stained-glass windows. I didn't care for church—I thought the services were boring and too long, and I had to attend both Sunday school *and* church. My mother certainly did her best if exposure counts, for I was surely exposed.

We lived in Clearwater during World War II. In Tampa, a few miles away, were two large Army

Air Corps bases. The pilots would fly out over the bay, across our beach, and then come flat-hatting in over the Gulf, three feet off the water—just enough to clear the jetties—and boy! this sure impressed me! I even learned of a mid-air collision over Clearwater, with parts of the airplanes dropping into the town! I was too young to grasp the tragedy of such a situation . . . all I could feel was the tremendous excitement of it. There is no doubt that my first interest in flying began right there on the beaches of Clearwater. Anything else looked far less exciting to me at that point.

All in all, my life in Clearwater was interesting. I even enjoyed my part-time work: I stocked groceries in a supermarket, did janitorial work in a dime-store, and sold snakes, frogs, and white rats to a Ross Allen reptile-collecting station; I also made spare money by diving off piers. Soldiers would throw nickels and dimes into the Gulf, and I'd dive off the roof of a twenty-foot pier, timing myself carefully, to catch the money under the water before it hit the bottom.

Those were good days—fun days—and we remained in Clearwater until I was in the seventh grade, when we moved to Oberlin, Ohio, under hopeful circumstances that didn't work out.

Dad had been in the Army in Alaska and had supposedly solved his drinking problem. He'd been recommended for Officers Candidate School in Miami and had graduated high in his class. Mother, of course, was very pleased and hopeful, and welcomed Dad back into the family. I remember looking at my father and thinking about him objectively—he was really a stranger to me—and feeling that he seemed like a pretty good guy with a lot on the ball.

After receiving his commission, Dad was stationed, coincidentally enough, at one of the Army Air Corps bases in Tampa. We'd moved from the beach to the outskirts of town, but, other than that, and having a father around the house, our routine changed very little.

Unfortunately, Dad's problem wasn't solved at all, and he was released from the Army. Doing her best to hold the family together, Mother agreed to move to Oberlin, Ohio, where Dad could be near his father and perhaps straighten out and find a good job. Within a year, however, Mother and Dad were divorced, and we returned to our old house in Clearwater, which had not yet been sold.

Our only reason for moving back to Clearwater was to sell the house, because my mother wanted an Ohio education for her children. A sale was arranged, and we stayed in Clearwater just long enough for the school year to finish (I was in the eighth grade). Then we returned to Oberlin, where Mother and Connie live to this day. At long last we had a permanent home, and things began to settle into a normal routine.

My mother had a remarkable facility for taking and keeping pictures of us when we were young, and my wife, Chris, whenever she looks at the old albums, has a way of pointing out how much better my mother looks today than she did during those days in Clearwater. She's not talking about the rough life my mother had with my father, but about the rough life she had with *me!* And she's not kidding.

For example, during the time we'd moved back to Clearwater to sell the house, I built a tree hut in a thirty-foot pine tree. To reach the hut, I built steps on another nearby tree, then extended a narrow bamboo walkway across the open space to the hut. At least once, I remember my brother and myself scooting up to the hut when we were supposed to be getting ready for Sunday school. There was my mother on the ground, dutifully calling us at the top of her lungs, while my brother and I chuckled to ourselves up in the tree.

If I had ever fallen out of that tree, I would have started my flying career a lot earlier!

Luckily, I didn't.

And, also luckily, I was beginning to outgrow such irresponsibility by the time we settled in Oberlin. The experiences and decisions that turned me toward a flying career—and all that has gone with it—were not far off as I prepared to enter my first year of high school.

3

Flying Lessons

ONE OF THE blessings of being a teen-ager is the growing awareness of passing from childhood— when so many, many things are beyond reach—to an age when at least some of the things you've always wanted to try are finally possible. In Clearwater, for example, I was much too young actually to fly an airplane, and the best I could do was hope that someday I might be a pilot. As a teen-ager, however (in my junior year of high school), I was old enough to take flying lessons and *be* a pilot.

I can't say, however, that the thought of flying dominated me. For example, I didn't build model airplanes, or collect them, or bury my nose in flying magazines, or anything like that. Even if I had, there still would have been the problem of time and expense. School and a job were two necessities of life by this time, and I considered these as part of growing up. When I did think about flying, it was as an interesting idea—something I'd like to do—but I didn't have any serious thoughts about it as a career.

The spark—if there was a spark—that finally put me behind the controls of an airplane may have been struck by watching an air show, or from casual conversation with friends. It always bothered me when people said how nice it would be to do this or that, but never did it. This really used to start me thinking, especially if the thing they wanted to do was easily within reach. It was likely after one of these go-rounds with my friends that I decided once and for all to take flying lessons at Coates Flying Service in nearby Elyria.

My first lesson was in an old Aeronca. If I live to be a hundred, I'll never forget the excitement I felt at actually handling the controls of an airplane and making it go where I wanted it to. Everything I'd ever dreamed about flying was true. This was a new and exciting realm. As the earth receded below me, and cities and men assumed tiny proportions in relation to the immensity of the open sky around me, I was distinctly conscious of a feeling that almost every pilot has experienced . . . a strange and almost startling closeness to God. The day-to-day frustrations of earth-bound life, the picayune problems and foolishness we all seem to be so involved in . . . none of these were present in the little yellow Aeronca as I winged my way high over the ground.

All of these sensations come tumbling into the new pilot's consciousness from his very first flight. I remember that in later years, when I was a flight instructor, I'd sometimes have to snap my students out of their reverie and put their minds back on the job at hand—flying the airplane!

The most important moment in a student pilot's life, of course, is when he solos . . . and it happened to me just about the way it happens to every student. After eight or nine hours of instruction, and some final landings and take-offs, the instructor casually steps out of the airplane—without shutting off the engine—then leans back into the cockpit and says, "She's yours! Try not to hit the wires when you're coming in!"

Then he strides off the field nonchalantly and leaves you sitting there in an airplane that looks mighty darned empty! This is the moment you've waited for, and you try to keep down the excitement as you turn around and taxi back to the beginning of the runway. "The airplane is lighter, now," you tell yourself, "so I have to adjust my trim." Then you make the most careful preflight cockpit check you'll ever make in your life, to be sure all the knobs and buttons and dials are where they ought to be.

Then you "pour on the coal" and *go!*

There's no turning back. The runway comes to an end beneath you, and you recall the old pilot's saying: *"The three most useless things in the world to a pilot are the runway behind him, the altitude above him, and the gasoline he's already used."*

Now you're at 400 feet and making a left turn to leave the immediate airport area (the plane is lighter than you'd expected without the weight of the instructor and responds more swiftly to the controls). You head away from the airport for about a mile, then turn back into the pattern (all you're expected to do on this first solo flight is to get this crate back on the ground in one piece).

Back in the pattern now . . . the turn into the runway coming up fast (watch the wires!) . . . she'll flare out more because she's lighter . . . flare out! . . . we're on the ground and rolling nicely!

Then you taxi over to the apron, and the instructor comes out with a big grin on his face and shakes your hand.

"Nothing to it," you say calmly . . . but inside you're as pleased as if you'd just conquered Mount Everest.

I soloed a few more times, but the expense of flying lessons was too much. I simply didn't have the money to spend like that. Older people—people I respected highly—had made it plain to me that I needed a college education if I were ever to get anywhere, especially since my interests were along math and science lines. Success in these fields demands college training, and I needed to save my money for continuing my education.

I still wasn't thinking of flying as a career, but more as a sport and hobby. As a matter of fact, when I went to the University of Colorado, I majored in *civil* engineering, rather than aeronautical engineering, which shows how far I was from considering a flying career seriously.

For these reasons, then, and with considerable reluctance, I had to make the hard decision to give up my flying lessons. I figured I would eventually be drafted, and I had some vague notion that the military would either teach me to fly or provide for my lessons after I was discharged. Nothing was very sure for me at that time, except that I had to keep up my "B" average in school and earn as much money as possible in preparation for entering college the following year.

And earn money I did. During my last two years in high school—after having worked for the Oberlin College maintenance department, repairing roofs, and also for a Jack-of-all-trades around town, repairing barns and homes, and doing all sorts of useful odd jobs—I went into business for myself, pruning trees (it wasn't flying, but it was at least up in the air!), doing some carpentry, painting, and other maintenance jobs in the area. In the summer before I went to college, I earned well over a thousand dollars.

It might sound as if I didn't have much time for high-school sports, but this was not the case. I earned letters three years in football, two years in basketball, and one year in track. I attached a great deal of significance to proper physical conditioning, which is probably one reason why to this day I don't smoke.

Another activity for which I always found time was Sunday school and church—and the group functions—at the local Methodist Church under the pastorate of Reverend Goist. That may sound odd after hearing about my lack of enthusiasm for church in Clearwater, but now I was older and Reverend Goist was special. He had a wonderful way with young people, and it was through him that I first began to understand something meaningful about religion, especially regarding the right and wrong rules for living. Get-togethers at the church were always wholesome and fun, and a good percentage of my friends felt the same way. When I finally got to college, I had the tendency, common to most freshmen, of trying to act a little "smarter" than I was. Despite this, I continued to attend church, and it constantly became more significant to me, thanks to the understanding and lasting groundwork laid by Reverend Goist.

During that last summer before entering college, I still didn't know what I wanted to do for my life's work. I didn't know what college I wanted to attend; I wasn't even sure what line of education I wanted to pursue. For some of the reasons mentioned earlier, I finally settled on an engineering career (I didn't know what kind of engineering I'd choose) and was accepted by several schools—one of which I had never even applied to! I don't know how in the world it could have happened, but I got a nice letter from Rice telling me that they had reviewed my marks, etc., and were delighted that I had selected their school!

I finally chose the University of Colorado. I had lived in the East (North and South), but never in the West, and I wanted to see what the people out there were like. The University of Colorado sounded like a nice sort of cowboy school, and I thought I'd probably like such an atmosphere. All of this makes about as much sense as flipping a coin, but that's the way I finally came to choose Colorado.

One factor which did affect my decision was my concern about being drafted before I could complete my education. I felt I had to go to a school that offered an R.O.T.C. (Reserve Officers' Training Corps) program, and Colorado offered all three of them: Army, Navy, and Air Force.

So, with suitcase and raincoat in hand, I hitch-hiked to Colorado. I didn't know it, but I was taking the first big step toward my naval aviation career.

4

Easy Decisions

WHEN I ARRIVED at the University of Colorado and checked over the R.O.T.C. programs, it became obvious to me that the Navy program was the one I wanted. The Army and Air Force seemed willing to accept any applicant, but the Navy people were not so eager. They insisted upon a test and then a further interview before they'd make a decision. This impressed me, and I just naturally felt they must have a better organization than the other services.

That was the first easy decision I made—to try my best to get into the Naval R.O.T.C. Fortunately, I passed the tests and became a "contract" student. The term "contract" means just what it says. I was on contract to the Navy to complete special courses in naval science during my college years, to make a cruise with them between my junior and senior years, and to spend two years on active duty after the completion of my courses. In return, I would be paid forty dollars a month toward tuition, room and board, books, etc., during my junior and senior years, and would eventually receive a reserve commission as an ensign.

Shortly after being accepted in the Naval program, I learned that the Navy had another program in operation that would enable me to become a commissioned officer in the *Regular* Navy after graduation. I preferred the *regular* status, feeling that it carried more meaning and certain financial benefits that would help me greatly during my college years. It would be necessary to spend four years on active duty with the Navy upon graduation, and to go on a cruise between each school year. I felt it was worth it, and put in my application.

This was another easy decision to make—but the test they gave me was the roughest and most difficult test I had ever encountered anywhere! It was really a bear. This was followed by further interviews, medical and psychological testing, and what-have-you. The Navy just wasn't kidding when it said you had to earn the right to join them; and I was mighty relieved when I "lucked out" on all the tests and was accepted.

Thanks to this Regular Navy program, I was now on a full scholarship to the university, with fifty dollars every month toward room and board. In addition, I had a series of jobs—waiting on tables, dishwashing, cooking—so that, when totaled up, it represented a profit above all major costs of between $50 and $100 a month.

Between my freshman and sophomore years I took my first cruise in the Navy—on the battleship *Iowa*—and I sure didn't have any trouble making another important decision: the ship-type Navy was not going to be my career! I would stay in for my obligated service time, but walking slant-legged along sloping ship decks and staring at a million miles of watery nothingness wasn't for me. There was plenty to keep me busy aboard ship, but the fact of the matter was that shipboard life left me unmotivated. This was my first experience with a battleship, and I wasn't even mildly excited. So that was out.

The following summer, between my sophomore and junior years, I was assigned another tour of duty with the Navy, not a sea cruise this time, but a familiarization and indoctrination program that took me to Little Creek, Virginia, and Corpus Christi, Texas.

And things *really* started to happen!

As soon as I left college at the end of my sophomore year, I hitchhiked home to take care of some repairs around the house. Being the older son in the family, these jobs naturally fell to me. Happily, I enjoyed any kind of carpentry or maintenance work.

I finished my chores and hitchhiked down to Corpus Christi, Texas, to report for what I had been told was an aviation indoctrination program.

This was part of the Navy's attempt to familiarize us with all branches of the service. I looked forward to it, but after my experience on the *Iowa*, I can't say I was expecting too much.

Incidentally, this passion I had for hitchhiking everywhere was mainly a method of saving money, but it had another odd effect on my life. When I first got to Colorado, I still hadn't made up my mind what kind of engineering course I wanted to take. I figured, however, that since I'd walked and ridden over countless bridges and roads, this was probably the only kind of engineering I knew anything about, so I chose civil engineering!

Anyway, down I went to Corpus Christi via the "thumb" method, fattening up my savings account with the travel pay the Navy had given me. Waiting for me at the end of my trip was my first ride in a military airplane!

All of us in this Naval program were midshipmen, the same rank as students at the Naval Academy in Annapolis. Each of us was scheduled for an airplane ride during this phase of our indoctrination to see if naval aviation appealed to any of us.

Well, when they walked us out on that big airfield, and I saw those SNJ's (propeller-driven naval trainers) lined up for what looked like a mile, my interest in the Navy went up a million points! I suited up, climbed into the airplane with the instructor, and I don't believe we were a hundred feet off the ground before I asked if I could try the controls.

Boy! The feel of that big engine (compared to the Aeronca) was just unbelievable, and I must say my instructor was a superagreeable fellow. He let me try anything I wanted, and I horsed that SNJ all over the sky. At one point I tried a loop—a maneuver I had only seen from the ground. I didn't know how the airplane should *feel* during a loop, nor where the controls should be, and I got us into such a steep nose-down attitude I thought the instructor would have to pull the wings off the airplane to get us out of it! I'm very happy to report that the wings stayed on!

That was really fun—but the best part was yet to come.

During our familiarization cycle at Corpus Christi, our indoctrination instructors asked for volunteers to ride the ejection-seat trainer. The ejection seat was set on vertical rails and had a reduced explosive charge in it. It was supposed to simulate an actual ejection from an airplane.

This looked like great fun to me . . . I thought it was better than a ride at a carnival, and, what's more, it was free! In fact, they were actually *paying* us for it! So I volunteered, and one other midshipman did the same. Wham! And up we went!

The lieutenant in charge of our group felt that

because we were the only two men in the group who volunteered to ride the ejection seat, we should get a reward.

So, reward us he did—with a ride in the T-33 jet trainer! A couple of days earlier, the only airplane I'd ever been in was an Aeronca, and now, all of a sudden, not only had I flown an SNJ, but coming up was a ride in the Navy's jet trainer. I felt the blessings had really been showered on me that day!

I was awestruck on that T-33 ride. What impressed me so much was the difference between a prop airplane and a jet. There was so little sound, and almost no sensation of speed. It was just as if we were suspended in space, and I again had that startling feeling of nearness to God. The whole ride made me feel a mixture of awe and inspiration—that's the only way I can describe my reaction. I remember the experience today as vividly as if it had happened yesterday.

The jet was so superior to the SNJ, at least in my opinion, that there was no question in my mind which I preferred . . . and, as a consequence of those two flights, I made up my mind that aviation was definitely the Navy duty I'd try for.

Of all the easy decisions I was to make during this period, the decision to choose naval aviation was by far the easiest.

They didn't have to ask me twice!

The rest of the tour that summer was anticlimactic for me. We moved on to Little Creek, Virginia, for amphibious indoctrination—climbing down cargo nets, familiarizing ourselves with assault boats, etc.—and the only part I enjoyed about this was that it was marine-type training, charging here and there and driving boats up onto the beach.

It was fun, but my enthusiasm was all for naval aviation.

I was hooked, but good.

5

Jet Pilot!

My JUNIOR year at Colorado was a difficult one. I was getting up early to cook breakfast for about 350 girls, studying late, and averaging about four hours sleep at night. It was inevitable that something had to give, and it turned out to be my math. I flunked a calculus course, and a passing grade in that subject was a prerequisite for other courses and for my civil-engineering degree.

As a consequence, I went to summer school that year, missing my cruise with the Navy and setting my commission back three months. Fortunately, however, my commission was back-dated to June, which meant I'd be promoted in the future along with the rest of my classmates. This left me with a favorable impression of Navy procedure.

I'd learned my lesson about working such long hours before and after classes, so, in my senior year, I worked just on weekends remodeling the dietician's cabin up in the mountains. I built an automobile bridge across a stream and a big stone fireplace, along with other interior work. This kind of work was right up my alley and it paid me just as much—more, in fact—than my former work in the kitchen of the girls' dormitory.

My luck held during my senior year, and I managed to graduate on time. After going on my "make-up" cruise, this time on the destroyer *Zellers,* I commenced my career in naval aviation. In September of 1956, right in the middle of hurricane Flossie, Ron Campbell and I reported for preflight training at Pensacola, Florida.

Ron had been a good friend of mine at college and a fellow midshipman in the Naval training program. We had similar interests; neither of us drank or smoked; and we were countrified—interested in the simple and sincere aspects of life. It was natural for us to "buddy up" in school and on cruises. Even though Ron had been assigned temporary Naval duty during that summer after our senior year, while I was making up the cruise I'd missed the year before, we managed to arrive in Pensacola together—in Levis and T-shirts.

The wooden B.O.Q. (Bachelor Officers' Quarters) we reported to was in possible danger of being blown apart by the hurricane, so we were hustled over to a sturdier looking brick building. This was fine, except that there was a lieutenant commander present who didn't at all like the idea of us being in Levis and T-shirts. He rose up from his chair and promptly "read us out" as we stood there dripping and trying to be respectful, telling us that if we wanted to be cowboys, we should have stayed in Colorado, etc., etc.

Fortunately for us, there was a commander present (I guess he must have been an ex-cowboy) who came to our rescue and told the lieutenant commander to sit down and let us alone. The commander also provided us with long-sleeved shirts from his room. We were told to join the others and eat, which we did, all the while casting furtive glances toward the lieutenant commander and hoping we weren't going to have to train under him.

That was our grand entrance into the Naval Air Training Command at Pensacola Naval Air Station. Ron and I had a talent for getting into *near* trouble—while always avoiding *real* trouble—and I'll tell about another funny incident we shared.

Preflight training, of course, involves only ground work—studies in navigation, engines, basic aerodynamics, and similar orientation—so it wasn't until we'd finished this phase that we actually began training in airplanes . . . the T-34, the Navy's primary propeller trainer.

Ron was assigned to another squadron during our T-34 syllabus, and because of variables in weather and training hours, etc., got a little ahead of me. We caught up with each other again at Whiting Field in nearby Milton, Florida, for our basic training in the larger prop-driven T-28. Ron had already had a few hops in the T-28, so he figured he just had to impress me.

The procedure for getting an airplane in those days was to walk out to the line, sign out the yellow sheet, preflight (inspect) the aircraft, and climb in . . . all of which Ron did, as nonchalantly as possible. He started up the engine, and, at an appropriate moment, I walked out, climbed aboard, and settled down into the rear cockpit.

Then off we went into the wild blue yonder for an hour or so of aerobatics and touch-and-go landings at a small, outlying field. On the way back, Ron remarked that there was something wrong—he didn't know what, but the airplane wasn't climbing as it should. I wasn't too worried, but Ron had signed for the airplane and he seemed somewhat concerned. Although I had never been in the airplane before, I thought I'd offer some helpful advice, and said: "Ron, if it's not gear, flaps, or speed brakes, I guess we're in trouble."

"You're right," said Ron, snapping his fingers. "It's the speed brakes. How did you guess that?"

"Superior flying ability, Clod," I replied.

The truth was that the T-34—the primary trainer I'd just graduated from—didn't even have speed brakes, so it was just a wild guess on my part. I just mentioned the only things I could think of that make an airplane sluggish and "dirty."

In any event, we got back safely, only to find

that the yellow sheet was gone. Actually, I had left the airplane practically before it stopped and had gone around the hangar and disappeared. As soon as Ron noted the absence of the yellow sheet, he just *knew* somebody had found out about our joy ride and had picked up the yellow sheet. At any instant he expected to be called into the office.

As it turned out, a student friend of ours had witnessed us getting aboard the airplane. Concerned that somebody else might also have had his eyes open, he had hidden the sheet until he personally could hand it to Ron. Too, I think he wanted us to worry a little.

Later, Ron and I exchanged some sighs of relief, realizing how close we'd come to maybe ruining a good part of our aviation future. Some aviators, just by their nature, have to get things out of their systems once in a while, and I think fate must allow them some early "forbidden" escapades.

After our fledgling days, we're on our own.

It was at Whiting Field, during my T-28 syllabus, that I met Chris, who was to become my wife.

One evening, Ron and I were in Milton . . . just looking . . . and we saw two young ladies get out of a car and go into the local theater. From our distance, the overall appearance of the girls was quite respectable. We went into a nearby restaurant and wrote a note on a napkin, giving our names, noting our fine caliber as Naval officers, our good, nondrinking, nonsmoking characters, and our interest in meeting some nice girls in Milton, rather than having to go all the way to Pensacola. We put down our address and phone number at the B.O.Q. and left the note in their car.

About ten days later, one of the girls timidly called, but, as luck would have it, I had another date on the only night we could arrange an introduction. I accompanied Ron to the meeting, however, and he obligingly visited with both of the girls that evening; he eventually wound up dating one of them fairly often.

I was still out in the cold, so to speak, but the sister of the girl Ron was dating was married to a Marine flight instructor; Ron and I enjoyed talking to him, and spent several evenings at his house. He had been in combat, and he had a good reputation for being an extremely capable and demanding instructor. He knew what pilots had to have in order to survive in combat, and, just by talking to him, I picked up a lot of useful information . . . including the name of a girl in Pensacola, Chris Robarts.

Actually, Ron's date, who had gone to Bible school with Chris in the ninth grade, told us that Chris would be just right for *Ron* (too tall for me), but that she'd surely have a nice friend for me.

We arranged to meet Chris; and when we did, I decided that I had never, in my whole life, seen anyone with such a sweet, innocent smile. All I could think about was beating Ron to the telephone after we left . . . which I did. Chris and I started dating. Chris didn't think much of me at first, but, with my great "charm and poise" (luck actually), I managed to win her admiration as time progressed.

It was just about that time that I was transferred to Barin Field in Foley, Alabama, for carrier qualification and gunnery training, the last step before entering advanced training, which I hoped would be in jets—the F-9.

Upon reporting to Barin Field, six of us rented an old farmhouse, and we were an interesting mixture. Ron and I, as usual, were the country folk, three of our fellow "farmhousers" were a wilder bunch of Indians, and the remaining member of the sextet was a serious, more reserved fellow on whom we would frequently play jokes, like hiding his car in the old barn or convincing him to call a local girl whom we had supposedly acquired as a date for him. When our housemate called the girl, I don't know who was more stunned, he or his pretended date.

All of us expressed our desire to get into jets during advanced training, but fate decreed otherwise. We all felt very bad when our serious pal was dropped out of flight training due to not meeting carrier-landing qualifications.

One of the other fellows, when it got right down to it, didn't want to remain in the Navy a moment longer than necessary; he quit flight training at the first opportunity.

This left Ron and me and the other two "wild Indians." We seemed to be equally motivated toward flying, and it was only pure luck that I was the one to be assigned to advanced training in jets, while the others got prop training.

When I passed my carrier qualification tests and gunnery—and I was no more than an average pilot at this stage, good in aerobatics, but weak on instruments—I was delighted to be assigned to the Naval Air Station in Memphis, Tennessee, for advanced training. This *assured* me of jets!

When Ron completed his basic flight training in the T-28, he was assigned to prop-driven A1H's—big, single-engine, lumbering, attack bombers. He's in a jet squadron today, but he was mighty unhappy about his prop assignment then, and, naturally, I wouldn't let him forget it! I remember we used to exchange letters after we got into advanced training. Mine were addressed (right on the envelope) as follows:

To: Lt. j.g. (very j.g.) Ronald K. "Clod" (Prop Driver) Campbell
From: Lt. j.g. Frank K. (Hot JET Pilot) Ellis

It had been a long time since I'd had that first T-33 ride in Corpus Christi, and it felt mighty good to be back in one, this time as a student with the prospect of being pilot-in-command in a very short time! The transition from props to jets was as wondrous as it had been the first time, and I knew way down inside that this was more than a passing phase with me; it was a very real love. It was about this time that I began thinking seriously of making the Navy a career. I knew it would be most disagreeable to have to leave these jets for an earthbound job.

The first phase of advanced training at Memphis consisted of advanced instrument work in the T-28, but that was over quickly, and the rest of my time in Memphis was solidly in jets. Actually, my entire time at Memphis, including the T-33 syllabus, lasted only about three months. I finished just before Christmas, bought a 1958 Chevrolet station wagon (future family planning!), and scooted home to Oberlin for the holidays (my hitchhiking days had ended). I then returned to the Naval Air Station in Pensacola to finish my advanced training in the Panther, the F9F-2 . . . though old, a real fighter type that made me undoubtedly the happiest guy alive!

The only cloud on the horizon was that a lot of pilots were being assigned to shipboard duty upon completion of their advanced training—and I don't mean in flying duties, but in general, *nonflying* duties!

This really concerned me, so I volunteered to be a flight instructor . . . and hoped!

6

A Familiar
Problem Begins

MY CAREER in the Navy has been marked by repeated efforts to remain in jets. Today, of course, as a double-amputee, this campaign has become tougher, but even in the early days I found I had to devote extra effort in an attempt to get jet rather than prop aircraft assignments, or, even worse, nonflying duties.

In this case, feeling I might be assigned to nonflying, shipboard duty, as some of my fellow students had been right after their advanced training, I immediately applied for the Training Command—to be an instructor. This would at least enable me to keep flying!

My first choice was to be an advanced instructor in the F-9 or T-33. My second choice was to be a basic instructor in the T-28 prop trainer—and that's what I got. Even though I'd lose out on jet time, I was at least building up valuable flight experience. And this tied in with another goal I had set my sights on—that of eventually becoming a Navy test pilot. The more flying time I could get under my belt, the better my chances of being accepted into the Navy's test-pilot school.

Essentially, then—just to sum up—I would have preferred carrier duty in jets, but there was nothing I could do to guarantee such an assignment. Next in line of choice was to be an advanced instructor in jets. Apparently, there was no billet available there, either, so I ended up as a basic flight instructor in the T-28.

One of my duties as a flight instructor was to fly "space patrol." As part of their training, students flew round-robin night hops. These were short flights, starting at Whiting, proceeding over several nearby towns, and returning to Whiting. At times it was possible to follow the airplanes' navigation lights around the entire course. Once in a while a student would get lost, or run into trouble, so an instructor would orbit each of the towns on the course to keep an eye on the students. This duty was called the "space patrol." I went on space patrol as often as possible to build up my night flying time, and some amusing things would sometimes happen up there.

For instance, there was the night one space-patrol flight instructor picked up the plaintive radio message: "Unidentified field, with unidentified aircraft landing, will you please identify yourself?"

He couldn't believe what he had heard . . . so he radioed another instructor on space patrol for confirmation. The other man had heard it all right; I think every instructor on space patrol that night burst out in hilarious laughter.

What had happened was this . . . a student had become lost, and had landed at one of Eglin Air Force Base's many fields. Not knowing where he was, he simply called the tower: *"Unidentified field, with unidentified aircraft landing, will you please identify yourself?"*

Well, the field identified itself, and an instructor who had heard the transmission radioed the student to stay where he was. Then the instructor flew to Whiting, picked up another instructor, and flew to Eglin to get the student out of his predicament. That radio communication ranks as a classic, even though, when one thinks about it seriously (hard to do), there really wasn't much else the student could have done under the circumstances.

A number of the instructors at Whiting at this time were fresh out of advanced training and had "plowed back" into the Training Command to rapidly build up flying time. First and foremost, they were spirited pilots who loved flying.

Chris and I had been dating regularly while I was at Whiting, and we were married on November 22, 1958, in the Pilgrim Church in Pensacola. I was a little better than halfway through my tour of duty as a flight instructor, and Chris was in nurse's training in Pensacola. We had some long talks about getting married at this time, and we both decided we'd be happier to do it then, Chris giving up her studies, and hoping we wouldn't need that education later on.

We started immediately to build a home—a little brick house at 16 Shady Lane in Milton, which we go back and look at every once in a while—and in the meantime, we lived in a little trailer behind a gas station. The cramped quarters probably contributed to the fact that I was a somewhat thoughtless husband during those first months of marriage —though I really blame it more on myself.

For too long a time after my marriage to Chris, flying was more important to me than anything else—as Chris will reluctantly avow when the subject is brought up. There were many nights when she sat alone in that little trailer, with supper getting cold, listening to the night-flying T-28's that sounded like a swarm of bees, and knowing that I was in one of the cockpits. I hadn't even been considerate enough to telephone her and mention that I wouldn't be home for dinner.

Chris, bless her, credited my thoughtlessness to the fact that I just wasn't used to being married and had forgotten to call—and that was giving me the benefit of the doubt if anyone ever did. Chris' strong religious background and even personality kept the peace in our family during those early months, and eventually I started to shape up and become more considerate and understanding. The birth of our first child helped me a lot, and, as with so many things in my life, this, too, took a somewhat unforeseen turn.

During her pregnancy, Chris was in the care of a country doctor in Milton. He was an outstanding doctor, and very dedicated, as he proved later; but when Chris started having labor pains one night— with the baby eight-and-a-half months along—I was concerned and telephoned him, and was a bit surprised by his somewhat casual manner.

"Now, now," he said, "this happens frequently. She's just imagining things. Go on back to sleep, and in a couple of hours everything will be okay."

We tried to follow his advice, but the pains kept getting worse and we couldn't wait a couple of hours. I called him again, and by this time it was in the wee hours of the morning.

"Well," he said, as seemingly casual as before, "it's too early for the baby." (He didn't know Chris had been water-skiing that afternoon and helping me pull weeds in the yard. She had taken the doctor literally about continuing her normal activities during pregnancy—why not!) "Anyway," said the doctor, "come on down and I'll give you some medicine for her."

So I went to the doctor's, dutifully brought the medicine back—which didn't help Chris at all— and called the doctor back a short time later.

"I'd sure feel better," I said, "if we went to the hospital. I don't know much about labor pains, but she's having them pretty regularly and not too far apart."

He agreed with me, out of pure weariness probably, because he didn't believe for a moment that Chris was ready to give birth, but he changed his mind fast when he checked her over.

"O-oo-o, yes!" he said. "You'd better *stay!*"

And stay I did, watching our first baby being born. When I went out to the squadron later that day to announce David's birth, the squadron C.O. looked at me and said, "You seem a little sober."

"Yes, sir. It was a sobering experience watching my first child's birth."

There was a brief pause while the officer reflected upon my statement. "You did wha-a-at?"

Meanwhile, back in the Training Command, I received orders to report to a heavy-attack squadron at Whidbey Island, Washington . . . I had heard that this new assignment might mean being a *bombardier-navigator*—not a pilot—for at least a year and a half.

With a feeling of foreboding, I called another instructor who'd gone to Whidbey a couple of months before, and I queried, "Bill, guess what I have orders to?"

Bill said, "O-h-h-h no, Frank!" Then he said, "Listen, I don't care what they tell you you'll be doing up here, it will be bombardier-navigator work—not piloting."

After that brief conversation, I realized it would be worth every effort on my part to get my orders changed. I had been hoping and *expecting* orders to a jet-fighter or light-attack squadron. And then *this!* It was a major disappointment.

At that time in the Navy, once a man was assigned to a coast, a detailer on that coast handled his assignment. Any changes in orders would have to be made through him.

This meant that the only person who could help me was a higher ranking officer whom I'd never met, who knew nothing about me, and who was 3,000 miles away on the Pacific Coast, with more important things to worry about than the reassignment of an unknown lieutenant junior grade in Florida.

So . . . I got my dimes out and did the only thing I could do. I called the AIRPAC assignment officer in San Diego, California.

7

Never Give Up!

"NEVER GIVE UP!" describes the attitude that has been a way of life for me . . . not only after my crash, but also before.

I remember one tragic incident that happened when I was stationed at NAS Miramar, just north of San Diego. It was a Friday afternoon. I'd finished my flying and other duties early, so I decided to head for home rather than sit around the squadron.

As I started to leave the squadron parking area, the crash crew came roaring up the street, sirens going, and up onto the "mat." I didn't think much about it, because any time a pilot declares an emergency, the crash crews came out all prepared —just in case. Usually it's something minor, and no serious problems are involved.

As I drove down the highway, I saw a big cloud of black smoke rising up from a mesa area adjacent to some residential housing, and I saw our two rescue helicopters circling the area. "Gee whiz," I thought to myself, "some poor guy's gone down in there, and maybe I'd better go over and check." So I drove toward the smoke and parked on a residential street as close to the scene of the crash as possible. Fire trucks, police, and residents of the area were all over the place.

I approached a policeman and told him I might be in the pilot's squadron, so he let me through. When I reached the end of the street, I saw a mass of people standing about on the edge of a gully. Something had obviously crashed in the gully. I asked some bystanders if the pilot had gotten out. They said, "We don't know . . . nobody's been able to get down in there yet."

"Has anyone tried?" I asked.

"Well, nobody can get down in there with all that smoke and fire," someone answered.

This answer made me so angry I could hardly see. Of all the people standing there—some of them in asbestos fire suits—apparently no one had attempted to go down and see if he could find the pilot!

Furious, I ran around to the other side of the mesa, where the fire had partially burned itself out, and made my way down into the gully toward the plane. Pieces of airplane were everywhere, and the smoke was much worse than the heat. I searched through the charred brush, and in a few moments I found the pilot. He wasn't a pretty

64

Toward the end of a perfect day.

With Chris, who has made all my family dreams come true.

My family—Chris, Debra, Dana, David, Daniel and me—enjoying bicycling together. (Danny and Dana are tucked nearly out of sight, in the picture at the top, behind Chris and me.)

After a little touch football, we go beachcombing—our preference is *family-type action!*

Four lively "stairsteps" keeping Dad in shape.

Getting set for some water-skiing.

"Rescuing a drowning shipmate" in the water-survival test.

Look, Ma, no legs!

Dunking by the Navy's water-survival "Dilbert Dunker."

Part of the frogman's obstacle course.

More of the obstacle course.

Proof of reaching the "summit"!

Talking airplanes with Captain Lester G. Radcliffe at Tripler Army Hospital in Honolulu. (To anyone who has been "through the mill," I say without qualification, "You *can* come back!") *Below:* Mutual of Omaha's Public Service Award. Left to right: Charles W. Mayo, myself, Lt. General (Ret.) Jimmy H. Doolittle and Mr. V. J. Schutt.

A very special moment—stepping forward to receive the Navy's Distinguished Flying Cross. (Chris is at the left; on the right is Vice Admiral Paul D. Stroop, Commander of Naval Air Forces, U.S. Pacific Fleet.)

My profession, my pleasure.

sight. He was one giant cinder, still strapped in his ejection seat. It appeared that he had not ejected, but gone in with the airplane.

I was ready to cry . . . for the pilot, for the smoke and the heat, and for the anger I felt because people hadn't even tried to get in and help this poor guy. They at least could have *tried!*

It might be argued—but not successfully in my presence—that there was nothing anybody could have done for that pilot, anyway.

Well, who *really* knows?

Anybody who had witnessed the crash that took my legs might have argued the same way, and I was far from being counted "out"—thanks to the prompt and effective action of the NAS Point Mugu crash crew and in particular one of the Navy crewmen, James Rubright, who rushed from the rescue helicopter, immediately removed his belt, and applied it to my amputated leg as a tourniquet.

The point is this: don't give up. It is inexcusable to make no attempt to save another human life, but it is also important to keep trying for success in every important venture. Defeatism, self-pity, considering something as obviously impossible and therefore not worth trying . . . these concepts are not worthy of a man. They're a sure route to ineffectiveness.

To get back to Whiting Field—after learning about my assignment to a bombardier-navigator tour, I did a little old-fashioned trying of my own on the phone with the AIRPAC assignment officer in San Diego. I told him who I was, that I was going to make the Navy my career, that I wanted to get to test-pilot school after this coming sea-duty tour, and I sure wasn't going to get there on bombardier-navigator crew time! I needed some first-pilot jet flight time . . . badly!

I experienced at that moment a combination of excitement and wonder. Here I was, asking a commander to permit me to plan my career in the Navy along the lines of my keenest motivation.

To my relief, he was very receptive. He asked me a lot of questions . . . where I'd gone to school, what I'd majored in . . . what I liked and what I didn't like . . . and so on. Then there was a quiet pause while he looked over his status board . . . and then. . . .

"Okay, Lieutenant, I'll send you to a fighter squadron at Miramar, California. You'll fly *Demons*. How's that?"

"Yes, *Sir*. Thank you. That's *great!*"

That's all it took—just directed motivation and one phone call. That was Friday afternoon, and by Monday morning I had a modification to my orders to report to the fighter squadron.

I was *deee*-lighted!

I finished my flight instructing; we made arrangements to sell our wonderful little brick house, packed ourselves into the '58 Chevy, and took off for San Diego, stopping en route to see my family in Oberlin and smiling all the way at the thought of flying those Demon jets.

We arrived in California in September of 1959. After hearing how beautiful California was supposed to be, we were disappointed to be greeted by parched desert. We managed to get into some apartment-type Navy housing, and, as far as living conditions were concerned, this was about the least pleasant we have experienced in my Navy career. However, flying the Demon was fun—it was a big, lumbering jet with an afterburner, supersonic if one went practically straight down—and I piled up considerable jet time during the six months we stayed at Miramar.

Our squadron was home-based at the Alameda Naval Air Station—just across the bay from San Francisco—for predeployment training (missile and rocket firing, intercept work, carrier qualifications, and other special training prior to going on a Pacific cruise aboard the U.S.S. *Midway*). The Demon was an all-weather night fighter, and it is generally agreed by pilots that night carrier landings are the ultimate in flying. Today, the carrier decks are lighted with floodlights, but then, in the "ancient days" of 1959 and 1960, the darkened ship had little runway lights, center-line lights, and threshold lights—not enough to illuminate

the deck, but just enough to show the runway out-
line. "Keep it lined up between the lights, boys!"
That was a real challenge and lots of fun.

I was going through my carrier-qualification
routine when Debbie, our second oldest child, was
about to be born. Commander Don Engen was
skipper of our fighter squadron, VF-21, at the
time. He called me in and said: "Frank, I know
what kind of a strain you're under with your baby
just about to be born, and there's no reason for
you to have to complete these carrier qualifications
at this time. There'll be nothing said, and no problems, and I'll certainly understand if you think it's
wiser to wait until after your wife has delivered."

Commander Engen was sincere, and I thanked
him for his understanding and concern. I told him
there was nothing to worry about. When I was flying carrier approaches, my mind was on my flying
and nothing else.

I went ahead with the qualifying, thinking, as I
do to this day, that Commander Engen is one of
the most outstanding men I've met in the Navy.

The following weekend we had a day's layoff
aboard the carrier, and the skipper suggested that
I take a Demon and fly to Alameda to see if everything was okay with Chris.

So, off I went in the Demon, straight to Alameda, about 400 miles away. Chris was surely surprised! That night I took her to the hospital to
have Debbie, got back in the airplane the next

morning, flew to San Diego, waited for the call to come back to the ship, then flew out and finished up my qualifying! It all worked beautifully, thanks to Commander Engen.

When the predeployment training was completed, our squadron went on a cruise to the southwest Pacific—where I got a greater appreciation of just how much of the earth is covered with water—and during our eight-month absence our home port was changed back to Miramar.

When I returned, Chris and I had to move back to the San Diego area, but this time we bought a nice little home in a new housing development.

There was some scuttlebutt around the squadron at this time that a couple of pilots would be transferred to the fleet replacement pilot training squadron, which meant that the pilots selected would be flying the new supersonic McDonnell F-4 Phantom. Also, it meant that, if chosen, I would be nearby for the birth of our third child.

So—zoom—I volunteered . . . and was selected. The actual assignment, however, was to a ferry squadron, VRF-32, at NAS North Island, just across the bay from San Diego.

The ferry squadron was just what the name implied, and my duties involved ferrying different types of aircraft around the country and from one coast to another. This duty boosted my chances for going on to test-pilot school, I felt, because I was then "current" in five different types of jet aircraft, including the F-4.

My sights were set even further ahead than test-pilot school, however; I ultimately hoped to get into the astronaut program. At this time, test-pilot experience was a requirement for the astronaut program, so I was more than ever determined to get into test-pilot school.

Commander Engen had already given me one fine recommendation to test-pilot school, and my skipper in the ferry squadron had given me another. As a matter of fact, while I was in the ferry squadron, I had the opportunity to fly to Washington a couple of times and talk with officers in the Bureau of Naval Personnel about my goals. It turned out that my rotation date—the date of my next assignment—was ripe for selection to post-graduate school, but bad for selection to test-pilot school. The assignment officer at the Navy Bureau of Personnel (BUPERS) felt that I'd be better off, and that my over-all Naval career would be enhanced, if I attended postgraduate school, but he left the decision to me.

I went back to North Island and thought about it long and hard, and then I wrote the assignment officer, Lieutenant Commander Bruce Bagwell, a long, personal letter, telling him I appreciated all the time and consideration I had been given, but felt I would be far happier going to test-pilot school because I wanted to get into the astronaut program. I also reiterated my concern with my rotation date.

I'll bet it wasn't more than three weeks later that I received a note from my detailer telling me my rotation date had been changed! And he ended by saying: "Good luck in the space program!"

If there ever was an example of the huge Navy machine—and especially the detailer in Washington—being considerate of one lieutenant (one of thousands!), that was certainly it!

At that moment, every indication pointed to my going on to test-pilot school—it looked like a sure bet—and hopefully into the astronaut program eventually.

I was easily the happiest guy alive.

Then . . . about two months later, July 11, 1962 . . . an unexpected thing happened to me in a Cougar jet as I came in for a landing at Point Mugu Naval Air Station. . . .

8

No Man Walks Alone

As FAR AS the Navy was concerned, the injuries I sustained in the Cougar accident finished me not only as a naval aviator, but also for the Navy itself. As soon as I was well enough to go home—so the feeling went—I would be discharged from the Navy with a medical disability. I'd be out. Medically retired.

As I was regaining my health in the Naval hospital in San Diego, I began to be aware of these views, and I knew I had to temper my confidence with proof. I never doubted for an instant that I could stay in the Navy and return to flying, but I then realized I'd have to fight hard against some outdated opinions that automatically labeled me "handicapped." I'd already tried on one temporary artificial leg hastily put together by a couple of corpsmen in the hospital, and although I was pretty weak, I felt that with better legs, and time to practice, I could serve the Navy as well as ever in the job I knew best. All I needed was a chance to show the Navy what I could do. First of all, this meant staying in the Navy and avoiding an automatic discharge.

Captain William S. Stryker—Chief of Orthopedic Surgery at the naval hospital in San Diego—gave me some *very* important help at this point. Mainly through his efforts, the Navy Bureau of Medicine and Surgery (BUMED) agreed to give me a medical survey as soon as Captain Stryker had fixed me up, fitted me with some good legs, and given me a chance to become accustomed to them. The feeling at BUMED was that I'd have the survey and then promptly be retired. But *our* feeling—Captain Stryker's and mine—was that the survey would show I was well enough to be returned to at least limited duty. Captain Stryker almost "lived" with me during those early days of recuperation, and he knew as well as I did that, with a little time, I would be able to perform a good job for the Navy and that it wouldn't help anyone to discharge me and put me "out to pasture."

With the medical survey facing me, I was determined to prepare myself in every way possible to prove to the Navy that I was still a mighty useful member of the group.

With a good artificial leg fitted to my right stump and a makeshift model (a plaster pylon) on my left, I returned home in November, less than four months after the accident. Initially, I was a little wobbly, but soon this ended, and I was driving our family car about two weeks later. On November 19, I reported for desk duty at the squadron office, but was able to work for a half day only because my back started hurting badly. By the month's end, I was able to work full time. Just before Christmas, my left stump was fitted with a finished prosthesis, and I walked without a cane or crutches for the first time since the accident. That was certainly a big day—one that left me with no doubt that I was on my way!

In January of 1963, about six months after the accident, I was given the promised medical survey in San Diego—and it was recommended that I be returned to active duty in a limited-duty status (back to the ferry squadron) and then given a more comprehensive medical survey in six months. This report was forwarded to Washington, and Captain Stryker and I were confident the recommendation would be accepted.

With two "good" legs under me, I *really* set about the job of proving that I was no more handicapped than the man in the moon—a place I still hope to walk around on one of these days. My diary shows that I rode my bicycle, played football with the children, marched in review, and handled my desk-bound squadron duties with increasingly less effort and pain.

While waiting for approval from Washington, I continued my efforts in San Diego . . . passed a flight physical, and also the naval aviator's water survival test. This test seemed little different than it had when I took it years earlier using my God-given legs; it consisted, in part, of being strapped into the mocked-up cockpit of an airplane (Dilbert Dunker) and then dunked upside down into a pool of cold water. The object is to get out and "survive." Other parts of the test included a dive from a twenty-foot tower and "rescuing" a fellow pilot who put a stranglehold on me. I left my "legs" at the side of the pool, feeling that it would be far more significant to try to pass the test on my "knees."

There was some newspaper and television publicity about the water survival test—some other fellows scheduled to take it that day had failed to do so because of very cold air and water temperatures, and our commanding officer was a little disgusted about it. He figured that if I could do it, then I should get some sort of publicity. I was given a swimming certificate, and the press was invited in to takes notes. From that time forward, I guess I became "news bait," for there have been numbers of stories written or told about the "courageous" Frank Ellis and his one-man fight with the Navy.

First of all, I'm not courageous; I just want to go back to work for the Navy to the fullest extent of my capability—no flight limitations. Secondly, this isn't a one-man fight against the Navy; my case involves a lot of highly trained people who are fighting *for* the Navy in an effort to demonstrate that some of the archaic thinking and opinions about the "handicapped" are really doing our military services more harm than good. At the very least, the military is losing a lot of good men whom it has trained and can use productively, and very often in the *same* job as before. There's a tremendous amount of needless waste of manpower involved in automatic decisions concerning the "handicapped."

In February—still waiting for the word from Washington—I visited other amputees in an effort to cheer them up. In the middle of the month, I took a short vacation to Hawaii with Chris and our two oldest children. We danced aboard ship—on a rolling sea—and, when we reached Hawaii, swam at Waikiki Beach to the accompaniment of stares from other bathers.

I couldn't keep out of airplanes, either; and in the early part of March, 1963, I spent a lot of time taxiing different kinds of aircraft. I had to develop a new technique or two, but nothing major, and there were no problems. Besides, I was in a nonflying category, and this was a chance at least to be inside an airplane. Later in March, I helped fly a C-47 cross-country on a ferry mission, and I remember returning from that flight thinking it was about time I heard from Washington.

Well, I heard from Washington, all right. The Bureau of Naval Personnel, due to recommendations from BUMED, was in total disagreement

with the recommendations that had been forwarded
from San Diego. They said it would not be necessary for me to be re-evaluated in six months, but I
was to remain on active duty for about twelve
months, during which I could adjust for retirement
to civilian life.

There it was . . . in black and white. Obviously,
the only thing to do was to keep trying, and find a
way to get to Washington and see somebody, or,
better still, several somebodies.

I didn't know *who* to see exactly, but I felt this
wasn't the end of my naval aviation career, just a
temporary setback, and I'd better do something
about it, because I sure hated to waste any more
time than necessary before getting back into a
flight status.

In Washington, I spoke to something like nine
admirals in one particular day, and finally presented my desires to the Secretary of the Navy,
Fred Korth. I made the trip with one basic goal in
mind—to demonstrate visible proof of my lack of
disability.

And . . . the trip paid off.

By the end of April, my squadron commanding
officer received a letter from Washington saying
they *agreed* I should be re-evaluated in a few
months! This was great! It was what I had been
"shooting" for since the accident, and I felt I'd be

able to pass any tests they gave me—which were then scheduled for July.

Bolstered by this good news, I "pulled out all the stops" to prove I was fit and able for anything. I negotiated most of the obstacles on the Frogman's underwater-demolition obstacle course. I climbed nets and ropes, scaled walls, etc. (Fortunately, news media provided plenty of pictures.) I went water-skiing, and finally completed what I felt would change the most fixed of outdated attitudes: I made a parachute jump—this time controlled.

I had a tough time convincing the San Diego Sky Divers' Club to let me step out of an airplane at 2,500 feet; but they finally relented, and out I went, twisting the foot of my right artificial leg to a 45-degree angle when I landed. That was easy to fix. I just sat down in the grass, twisted it back into place, and walked off the field. Other than that, no problems were encountered.

What I really was trying to do was to answer any doubts the Washington people had about my ability to cope with a complete Naval aviation career.

"Can you walk on a pitching deck?" might be one question.

"Yes, sir, and even dance on one!" (as I proved on my trip to Hawaii with Chris) was the kind of factual answer I had to be able to give. All of my efforts were devoted toward demonstrating that my physical capabilities were near normal and that my flying capabilities *were normal.*

They could say, "Lieutenant Ellis, you have two artificial legs. You *can't* perform physically as well as a man with two natural legs."

To that, I had to be able to say—with proof— "Whatever the Navy's physical regulations are for an aviator, I believe I can meet them. In regard to those regulations, I am not disabled. If there are some tests which I have not yet taken—because I haven't had the opportunity—my current abilities indicate that I should be given those tests."

In the evenings and on weekends during the time I was getting ready for the July medical re-evaluation, I put together a thick and imposing portfolio of letters, pictures, reports, and recommendations to carry to BUMED in Washington. Aside from actually flying an airplane alone to demonstrate my flight proficiency, which I wasn't allowed to do, I took every test available to me and demonstrated in every way possible that I had no physical limitations as a naval aviator.

The medical re-evaluation itself was the only remaining gap in my portfolio—and I filled that in in July. The local Board of Medical Survey recommended that I be returned to *full duty with no limitations*—a big step forward from the earlier report!

Accompanying this report was a flight physical, and it was recommended that I be put in Medical

Service Group III for a period of six months and then re-evaluated at the end of that time.

This meant *flying!* Medical Service Group III signified that I could fly only in dual-controlled aircraft with a qualified pilot in Group I (an unrestricted category)—but it was the first step toward resuming a flying career, and I was really pleased with the recommendation.

Normally, these recommendations and reports would have been delegated to a standard Navy form of several pages and forwarded to Washington. Considering the unusual nature of my case, however, I added the reports to my bulging portfolio and personally delivered everything to the proper people in Washington, again making the rounds and doing everything possible to convince my listeners that some of their ideas about the "handicapped" were outdated and that I, for one, should be allowed to fly.

Some months before going to Washington for the second time, I forwarded a letter to the Secretary of the Navy, via the chain of command, stating my desire to remain a naval aviator. This letter received extremely favorable endorsements locally —not so in Washington.

I was attacking on two fronts, so to speak, in an effort to cover all possible Navy avenues to success. While my portfolio was being reviewed by the Naval Bureau of Medicine, my letter to the Secretary of the Navy was also being read and passed along. As it turned out, the Bureau of Medicine and Surgery and the Bureau of Naval Personnel were still reluctant to return me to any sort of flying duty, but the letter to the Secretary, which had reached the office of the Chief of Naval Operations by this time, got favorable results!

On August 30, 1963—a year and a month after my crash—the Deputy Chief of Naval Operations (Air) issued an endorsement to my letter that admitted the wide diversity of medical opinion regarding my physical qualifications. But whereas the Bureau of Medicine and Surgery had recommended limited, nonflying duties, this endorsement placed me in a Group III flying status and directed that special physical tests be given me to determine my capabilities once and for all. The Bureau of Medicine and Surgery was directed to *"prescribe an appropriate group of physical tests, if these do not already exist, in order that it may be conclusively ascertained,* in all such cases, *whether or not a candidate is fit for all duties at sea and ashore with respect to his ability to perform duty involving flying."*

This letter came through to my commanding officer on September 18, and I jumped for joy!

I think the most important part of the endorsement was the phrase *in all such cases*. This was striking a strong blow for all the so-called "handicapped." It meant that Navy men who lost a leg or an arm, or were otherwise maimed, would have a chance to be judged according to their own individual merits and rehabilitation success.

It seemed as if a big hole had been knocked in a lot of ancient and harmful attitudes.

I was elated!

The period between the crash and my second medical survey certainly marks the most dramatic chapter in my recuperation. I was to continue improving, of course, but from being a "severely disabled" double-amputee to receiving orders for a return to Group III flight status took only fourteen months, and even that could have been shortened considerably.

Thanks are due to many, many people, both military and civilian, but there is no question in my mind that God has noticed and helped Frank Ellis.

There's nothing mystical nor complicated in my convictions. In the first place, God put nerve endings in exactly the right places for me to be able to use artificial legs. Secondly, He gave me total confidence that I would walk again and be able to perform as a man, as a father, and as a useful naval aviator. The spirit and the means were there—if I took advantage of them—to consider the loss of my legs as only a temporary setback, and certainly not as a permanent disability.

In all honesty, I can't sit back and state matter-of-factly that I wasn't killed in the crash *only* be-

cause of totally understandable circumstances . . .
the eucalyptus trees breaking my fall, for example.
Considering every known factor of the crash, I can
arrive at only one conclusion: in some way, God,
indeed, had a hand in my survival. There was a
purpose behind my survival, perhaps already ful-
filled, perhaps waiting for fulfillment in the future.
I frankly don't know.

But I have absolutely no doubt that whatever
that purpose is, it will be accomplished.

Call it faith, if you will . . . but no man walks
alone . . . and it is my personal conviction that God
will cast a helpful eye on any man who calls upon
Him in faith.

Conviction, determination, faith . . . these are
the fine parts of man, God within us; and if there
is tragedy and hopelessness in this world, it is because some men do not grasp these things and hold
on to them with a grip of iron.

Taken from you may be your arms, or your legs,
or your eyes . . . but you can never be defeated
while your conviction, determination, and faith
remain.

9

The Trouble
With Washington . . .

A SPECIAL BOARD of Flight Surgeons was convened in Pensacola to determine my physical capabilities and flying proficiency. I reported to the
Board in late October, 1963.

The medical evaluation included a water survival test, swimming, gymnasium exercises, and an
obstacle course. I experienced no unusual difficul-
ties in these tests, and the reports showed that my
physical abilities were normal for a naval aviator.

I especially looked forward to the flight evaluation tests; the first was in a T28B, reminding me
of my flight instructing days in Milton. I quote
from the check pilot's report:

> I consider Lt. Ellis to be fully possessed
> of the manual dexterity necessary for
> safe, coordinated flight and ground op-
> erations. He is, in fact, a fine aviator.

My next check-flight was in a TC-45J. In addition to a regular check, I was given special problems to show up any lack of leg movement. I was somewhat apprehensive about this flight in the TC-45J, because I had never made a landing or a take-off in this type of aircraft. My experience in the TC-45J amounted to only two or three hours in which I had merely controlled the airplane in flight. My apprehension changed to satisfaction, however, because the check pilot reported as follows:

> Considered above average for first attempt. It is my opinion that Lt. Ellis has both the judgment and capability to perform the technical and physical requirements for first pilot control of this aircraft.

The next airplane was a Cougar, similar to the one I had ejected from at Point Mugu. This was a seventy-minute flight, including aerobatics. The check pilot's report read:

> Lt. Ellis performed the maneuvers in a professional manner. His use of brakes and rudder was smooth and positive. His general airmanship was excellent in all respects. Ingress and egress (getting in

and out of the plane) were performed without the use of a ladder and with no difficulty being detected. . . . Lt. Ellis has demonstrated to my complete satisfaction his ability to solo the TF-9J. Judging from this officer's performance on the subject flight, I believe that any Check Pilot who lacked prior knowledge would be unable to detect that Lt. Ellis is a bilateral amputee.

The above report was especially significant to me, because the check pilot involved was Captain John Thomas, who had considerable jet-fighter experience. In fact, he had been the C.O. of the Demon Fleet Replacement Pilot Training Squadron to which I had been ordered at NAS Miramar in 1959 after getting my orders to the heavy attack squadron (bombardier-navigator duties) changed.

The flight tests were followed by a psychiatric examination and further interviewing; and from the individual reports to which I had been able to listen, I felt confident that I had demonstrated successfully my physical and flying abilities. This confidence was heightened by the final comments of the President of the Special Board of Flight Surgeons, Captain C. P. Phoebus. His written report represented a brave and firm stand, part of which reads:

Lt. Ellis is a truly unique individual in terms of his motivation, his determination and achievements in preparing himself for any and all duties of a Naval aviator in spite of his amputation handicap, and, last, but far from least, his superior physical condition. . . . From the physical examination standpoint, there is no question whatsoever of the fact that Lt. Ellis is fit in all respects for duty. . . . It is pertinent to note that, in a paradoxical way, Lt. Ellis with his artificial limbs stands in somewhat less danger of incapacitating injury through exposure to common hazards than does the normal pilot. Some of the most common disabling injuries to aviation personnel are those involving sprains, fractures, wounds, etc., of the lower extremity. In Ellis' case, these hazards do not exist. . . . From the flying viewpoint, the evidence presented to the Board indicated that Ellis, in spite of his handicap, is a superb pilot. His performance is above average in every respect, and there seems to be no reason to anticipate that he would be unable to carry out all of the duties of a Naval aviator in any kind of aircraft. Lt. Ellis' performance in the survival and physical fitness testing program indicates that one need have no fears for him in any emergency or survival situation that might arise. There is only one thing he cannot do as well as others, namely running. It was interesting to note that when this defect was mentioned during the course of the Board proceedings, Ellis' response was to the effect that he had not previously considered running as being of any particular importance. However, he will now concentrate on acquiring the skill . . . (and) . . . certainly his past performance in acquiring other skills would lead one to expect success in this endeavor.

Attached to this report was a recommendation that I be placed in Medical Service Group II, enabling me to fly with only one restriction—no carrier duty. I was pleased with the recommendation, because it meant that another big step had been taken toward my eventual return to an unrestricted flight status—or at least I thought so.

The recommendation, accompanied by all of the previous reports, was forwarded to the Bureau of Medicine and Surgery.

What happened next may seem somewhat unbelievable.

BUMED turned it down.

The Special Board of Flight Surgeons represented the Navy's "specialists" in aeromedicine. They had found me qualified for a Group II status, and it was inconceivable to me that BUMED in Washington would disregard their recommendation. The fact that BUMED did exactly that indicated plainly that I was a special case, in which the *attitude* of BUMED toward an amputee, rather than the demonstrated facts of his physical ability and flight proficiency, dictated their decision.

Fortunately, before I had left Pensacola, Admiral Lee had called me into his office and complimented me on my performance, telling me sincerely that if there ever was anything he could do for me, not to hesitate to ask.

I took him at his word; I telephoned him, told him what I had heard about BUMED's reluctance, and said that I'd be more than glad to come back to Pensacola and take the tests over again, including as many new ones as were deemed necessary. Admiral Lee was already aware of the problem, saying he didn't believe it would be necessary for me to take the tests again, because this appeared to be an administrative problem, solely—a matter of protocol, not further testing. It seemed obvious that I was qualified as far as the flight surgeons were concerned. The thing that had to be altered was Washington's adamant stand on the rule books —there were no provisions for bilateral-amputee naval pilots.

I was still considered "news bait" by the press, and articles about my efforts to regain an unrestricted flight status appeared frequently in magazines and newspapers, including a *Life* magazine story in October, just before I was evaluated in Pensacola. I've always had mixed feelings and considerable reluctance about the publicity, but letters and comments from other "handicapped" people attest that the articles about my efforts have been of help and encouragement to many. With that view in mind, I was honored to accept the Mutual of Omaha Insurance Company's Public Service Award in December of 1963. The most prized honor I received, of course, was the Distinguished Flying Cross for guiding my disabled Cougar away from the trailer park instead of immediately ejecting.

The awards . . . the publicity . . . all were appreciated. People just couldn't do enough kind things for me. But the one thing I was trying for the hardest I couldn't get—my old job as a fully qualified naval pilot. I was fully qualified, but I still didn't have the job.

In January of 1964, about two-and-a-half months after my tests in Pensacola, I arrived at NAS Jacksonville on a ferry flight (as copilot) in a multiengine P-2 patrol bomber, and found a message waiting for me to return to North Island immediately and then report to Pensacola for a second series of tests. Incidentally, I have a lot of respect for multiengine pilots—something I learned in Group III. Flying the big planes is like playing tackle on a football team—do all the work and get none of the credit; while flying the fighters is like being the halfback or quarterback—easier work and all the glory.

Anyway, whatever Admiral Lee and/or others had done, and whatever was going on in Washington, somebody was seeing to it that I had a second chance to convince the Navy that I belonged at least in Group II. I flew back to Pensacola as fast as wings could get me there.

Well aware of the behind-the-scenes problems I faced, Captain Phoebus gave me the opportunity to recommend the types of tests that I thought would finally convince the Bureau of Medicine and Surgery that I was not handicapped by anything except attitudes. Among other things, I suggested carrier landings, which they allowed me to make; the only request of mine I recall their turning down was making a parachute jump into the Gulf of Mexico as part of the water survival test.

It's not necessary to quote the reports on this second series of tests. It's enough to say that I improved on my previous performances, especially in regard to running. They put me through a particularly realistic survival training course. The route was carefully planned by a group of us to be one of the most difficult passages that could be found in the immediate area . . . and some of the details about this are interesting.

The instructors took me 175 yards offshore into the Gulf of Mexico. The water temperature was about 47° F, the air temperature 52° F, and the waves four to six feet high, with an outgoing tide. I wore a "wet" suit and a "Mae West," but no gloves. I jumped into the water, climbed aboard a small life raft, and made my way back to the beach against a wind of more than twenty miles an hour.

I crossed the beach, and then crawled and slopped my way through a lagoon, which was 100 yards of mud one to two feet deep, topped with thick sea grass. Major Spencer, who was hovering over me in a helicopter, said it was nearly impossible for anyone to walk or crawl in that lagoon.

After negotiating the lagoon, I crossed a small peninsula, a small island, and then a ship channel. The channel had a current flow of about eight miles an hour, and I was swept downcurrent about fifty yards.

After crossing the channel, I came up on the second beach and out onto a roadway, the end of the course.

It took me one hour and fifteen minutes to negotiate the entire course . . . and this, according to the written report filed by the instructors, *"is considered to be 20–30 minutes less than the time required by 70% to 80% of the students attending the course, even in good weather and ideal conditions."*

The flight tests were much more comprehensive than the ones I had in October. I had a total of eight flights, including one-and-a-half hours at night, seven night landings, thirty-eight day landings, four carrier landings, aerobatics, formation sequences, radio navigation, and instrument landings. I even had a helicopter flight to determine my ability to mount and dismount this type of aircraft. (No problems.)

I received excellent reports on all my flights, and one check pilot stated: "I could find nothing in this flight to separate Lt. Ellis from the average aviator except the fact that he is slightly above average for his present level of proficiency."

The Special Board of Flight Surgeons prepared the final report, which stated that I could fly as well as or better than the average pilot of my experience, that I could compete with my contemporaries in every reasonable physical and survival test situation, and that the Board found me fit for duty involving flying—so much so, in fact, that some of the Board members felt I was qualified for the unrestricted Group I status. The Chief of Orthopedic Surgery, Dr. Hemness, who had felt in October that I was *not* fit for flying duty, changed his mind one-hundred percent this time and voted for my receiving a Group I rating!

I had done everything I could. I knew I had

10

Take It Easy, Ellis

THE DECISION by the Special Board of Flight Surgeons in Pensacola, retaining me in a Group III status, was the biggest disappointment in my career.

But I was more than disappointed. I was furious . . . disgusted . . . unbelieving. I realized angrily that I was fighting shadows, outdated concepts, automatic decisions regarding the handicapped . . . and a host of "what if" problems: What if Lt. Ellis had to eject from a supersonic jet? What if Lt. Ellis had to sprint across a flight-deck in an emergency? What if Lt. Ellis couldn't get on the brakes fast enough to avoid taxiing into a crewman on a carrier flight-deck? "What if . . . what if?"

Most of the "what if" problems apply equally to every aviator in the Navy. Others are definitely in my favor. In survival situations, for example, I'm less susceptible to frostbite or snakebite, and, as the Board report stated, I would be less prone to disabling injuries in the lower extremity. As every test proved, without question, my chances and performance in any situation are on a par with my fellow Navy fliers. The check pilots who rode with me had no doubts about my performance on the brakes. For the life of me, I can't see any differences between my ejecting from an aircraft at supersonic speeds and anyone else's. As a matter of fact, I've got less of me to be injured, and I might very well fare better!

As for sprinting across a flight-deck, that is a legitimate "what if" . . . but not to the extent that I would get in someone's way or endanger other crewmen. My running abilities have improved steadily, and I'm sure they fall well within the minimum desired.

It was a silly thought—prompted by anger, I'm sure—but as I stood there in disbelief at the recommendation of Group III flight status, I gladly would have "taken on" the Board man by man, or all of them at the same time. I felt, "What a display of lack of courage and faith . . . afraid of public reaction if I had another accident . . . afraid of what their superiors at BUMED would say . . . afraid of who-knows-what-else."

My immediate notion was to grab the nearest telephone and call the Undersecretary of the Navy, Paul Fay, who was the highest ranking Navy person in favor of my campaign. I knew how upset I was, however, so I decided to cool down before calling him. I flew back to San Diego, and waited two weeks—I was still just as steamed up as before, so I called him.

I told him exactly what I thought about the whole situation, not mincing any words, and he promised to make a complete review of my case. It didn't help any to read press clippings which hailed me as the first double-amputee to remain as a military flyer in the history of the United States. True, I was in Group III, and able to "sit in" as copilot or accompany Group I pilots when the situation presented itself, but I felt I had proved my way to a better status. Not only was I "way down the ladder" as far as flying was concerned, but then there seemed to be little chance of reaching test-pilot school and the astronaut program. Actually, the enthusiasm I had for going into these more demanding flying duties was one of the reasons the Board put forward for keeping me in Group III— "to protect Lt. Ellis against his own ambitions"!

"Come on, be realistic!" I thought to myself as I looked over the report.

Mr. Fay telephoned me at the squadron a month later, and said he had decided to approve Group III status . . . and for some of the reasons mentioned earlier, such as the tight taxiing on aircraft carrier decks, the adverse publicity the Navy would suffer if I ever got into another accident, and because it wasn't right to subject my family to the possibility of a similar situation in the future.

Although I partially concurred about the adverse-publicity matter, I felt the remainder of the objections were baseless, especially the part about subjecting my family to possible further grief. (That is strictly a personal matter, of which my wife and I are the best judges, and she is my strongest supporter in my efforts to regain unrestricted flight status.) Keeping me in Group III was clearly a policy decision as far as I could determine, and although I disagreed with it, I thought very highly of Mr. Fay for telephoning me and telling me in a straightforward manner just what the problems were.

Several other influential persons took up my cause in Washington, particularly U.S. Congressman Charles A. Mosher, who lived in my home town of Oberlin, Ohio. Despite the very able efforts which Congressman Mosher and many others put forth on my behalf, the end result remained Group III. This was my destiny at that moment.

There was only one thing to do . . . cool down and bide my time until another opportunity presented itself to try for a better status.

I thought perhaps my best course of action would be to attend the Naval postgraduate school in Monterey, California. My Group III status effectively washed out any immediate chances to attend test-pilot school. Studying at the Naval postgraduate school would give me three years to improve my walking and perhaps get new and better legs; certainly, further education would advance my Naval career more effectively than an assignment to a desk job somewhere.

Perhaps during the time I attended postgraduate school, some of the Navy's attitudes would change. I'd have opportunities to speak to groups, and to prove again and again that I had a disability in name only. I felt this attitude-changing project might take some time—a considerable amount of time, if judged by my recent frustrating experiences. I thought that the best way to spend my time would be in working for a Master's degree in aeronautical engineering. At least I wouldn't be going backwards!

The single brightest light during this period shone in the form of our fourth little "D." On September 12, 1963 Danny was born in the same Coronado hospital where Dana arrived.

Fortunately, I *was* selected for postgraduate school, so, in the summer of 1964, Chris, the children, and I moved into a pleasant little home in a quiet section of Monterey; and I started attending school in August.

The three years we spent in Monterey were not the happiest of my life—the *long* study hours were made tolerable by a wonderful family, excellent living conditions, and the opportunity to fly twice a month in single-engine prop or jet aircraft—but

I dedicated myself to learning what I could. I am far from being the best of students, and I have never felt that education per se proves much. It becomes meaningful when you can apply it, though, so I found my engineering studies leaning more and more toward the analysis of structures and problems regarding artificial legs.

My thesis, as a matter of fact, when I graduated in 1967, was titled: "Below Knee Prosthesis Design Considerations." An interviewer once asked me what in the world a thesis on that subject had to do with obtaining a Master of Science degree in aeronautical engineering!

Actually, there are similar factors in the construction of an artificial limb, particularly a leg, and in the construction of an airplane. For example, the problem of load transfer from the landing gear of an airplane to the fuselage is related in some ways to load transfer from an artificial leg to the remaining stump. Countless variables in limb design occur due to stump change in varying weather conditions, personal likes and dislikes, comforts and discomforts, and needs of the wearer in relation to his weight, balance, and planned activities. Not all of these factors are related to aircraft design problems, but they are surely just as complex.

My personal experience formed the basis of the thesis, of course, and this was supplemented by a great deal of discussion, observation, and help from doctors and prosthetists (specialists who build artificial limbs).

As I look back on my three years in Monterey, I know I learned, and I hope I contributed, some new and worthwhile concepts on the whole large problem of attitudes and opinions in regard to the amputee. I did, indeed, have many chances to accept public-speaking requests, which gave me the opportunity to present my views nationally.

I also learned a few things about aeronautical engineering . . . a good academic background for becoming an astronaut.

I hadn't forgotten about the astronaut program.

Not for a minute.

11

Apollo

WHILE AT MONTEREY, I became aware of the fact that NASA was going to select candidates for the Apollo program. I obtained a copy of the requirements, and, lo and behold, there was nothing in those requirements that would preclude my applying. In fact, I met all the requirements listed. Although it certainly would have helped my cause to have been a graduate of the Navy's test-pilot school, there was no regulation that prevented a Group III naval aviator from trying to join the moon-bound team.

With a growing feeling that this time something was really going to happen, I called my Navy assignment officer in Washington and told him that I intended to apply for the Apollo program if there were no rules precluding such an application.

"Oh, my gosh," he chuckled, fairly familiar by this time with my ambitions. "Gee, Frank, I don't know. But I'll look into it, and you call me back next week."

I called him as requested, and he said he couldn't find a thing—there was nothing in the regulations to prohibit my application; and if I wanted to follow through, I was free to do so.

One of the requirements was that a candidate had to be less than six feet tall. That was no problem, of course. With my artificial legs on, I'm about 5 feet 10 inches tall. However, I felt I had a singularly attractive feature to offer the space-capsule designers—my height is adjustable to their needs. So, for the item on height, I wrote "adjustable from 4 feet 11 inches, knee-walking, to anything desired, wearing prostheses."

Naturally, I didn't just "fire off" the application and let it go at that. I was afraid the old attitudes would automatically dictate a negative reply, so I accompanied my application with medical reports, recommendations, and other pertinent data.

After the Bureau of Naval Personnel convened their Board to select the candidates whose names would be submitted to NASA, I learned—glory be!—that my name was among the fifty or so selected! No special consideration had been given to me; I was simply one of the many who met all the requirements. But my name was on that list!

Well . . . someone in the Bureau of Naval Personnel had second thoughts about this and called the Manned Spacecraft Center to be sure that the inclusion of my name on the list wouldn't embarrass NASA.

"Not at all," was the answer. "If you feel Ellis is qualified, then by all means keep his name on the list."

Next, the list was sent to the Chief of Naval Operations (CNO) for approval. My name was no longer included. This fact apparently aroused the interest of at least one admiral who was aware that I had been originally selected. Though my name was not returned to the recommendation list, Admiral McDonald, CNO, did append a letter to the list sent to NASA. It read, in effect, that Lt. Ellis was not technically qualified for the astronaut program, but from the standpoint of motivation, background, training, and experience, *would have rated No. 5 on this list.* It was requested that he be given special consideration for employment in any appropriate capacity.

News of this action reached the news media, and I began getting considerable publicity and even some congratulatory mail from folks who thought I'd made the astronaut program. During this period, Mr. Mosher, with his continuing interest in my case, wrote to Mr. Webb, Director of NASA, in my behalf. (In one of my letters to Representative Mosher, I mentioned that one orbit around the earth by a double-amputee would do more to further the goals of the President's Committee for Employment of the Handicapped than many years of the presently employed methods for educating the public along these lines.)

CNO's gesture was most considerate, but it left NASA with but one choice—not to consider Lt. Ellis for astronaut training. NASA has exceedingly stringent requirements for its pilot-astronauts—far tougher requirements than those for a naval aviator—and the Navy's refusal to upgrade my group status, plus the fact that I was "technically" not qualified (plastic legs), ended the matter right then and there.

And there it has remained ever since.

You know, I honestly believe I could have had a fighting chance at the program if I had been judged on my performance and abilities rather than prejudged by attitudes out of the "dark ages" in regard to my terrible "handicap."

After that disappointment, and reflecting on the Navy's reluctance to allow me to fly to the maximum of my motivation and capabilities, I decided to write to other organizations to see if it was just the Navy, or if others, too, would limit my flying. I wrote to NASA and asked them about the possibilities of becoming a *civilian* research test pilot. This was the first time I had given any thought to leaving the Navy, but I didn't feel I had much choice. I'd been trained as a pilot, all my interests and motivations were along that line, and I was at least as proficient in my trade as others with similar training. Not being allowed to progress in flying was equivalent to losing my career.

When I wrote to NASA, I fully expected to get back the same familiar, polite refusal that ". . . due to medical reasons, we are sorry to tell you, etc. . . ."

But not so this time. I got back "eligible" ratings. No restrictions of any kind were indicated from the boards of examiners at Houston MSC, Edwards AFB, and Moffett Field, though the letters made it clear that it might be some time before an appropriate opening would be available. That was in December, 1966; and, so far, nothing further has occurred. Becoming a research pilot for NASA, of course, could help move me toward eventually becoming a civilian astronaut—one of the principal reasons I applied to them.

But, aside from becoming an astronaut, I wanted to continue my flying and to progress as much as possible. With this in mind, I began to contact aircraft manufacturers and airlines, writing letters applying for test-pilot or just general piloting positions.

As you might expect, most of my applications met with a polite "thumbs down." In some cases, the principal reason I could not get a position was that the aircraft manufacturer was on contract to the government, and its choice of test pilots was closely supervised by the Navy or Air Force. In these instances, my Group III status "shot me down" immediately.

The negative replies from the airlines left a little more to be assumed. Their test pilots are usually their regular "line" pilots, and their public-relations people probably had heart attacks at the mere thought of my becoming a copilot or captain for regular commercial flights.

My primary effort is still directed toward upgrading my medical service group status in the Navy. I want very much to stay in the Navy—if I am permitted to progress according to my *demonstrated* flying abilities.

As for civilian employment, my target is still NASA—or some other Federally sponsored test facility free of any direction from the Bureau of Medicine and Surgery. If there is a pilot opening in such a facility and I'm offered a job where I can perform as required, I'll request to retire from the Navy.

In July of 1967, I was graduated from the U.S. Naval Post Graduate School in Monterey, and was assigned to the Naval Air Rework Facility, NAS Jacksonville, Florida.

That's where I am now—behind a desk.

In the final report by the Special Board of Flight Surgeons in Pensacola—written after my second evaluation—there is an interesting paragraph which states that I might ultimately requalify for unrestricted flight duties, but that I should approach this objective gradually—i.e., ". . . *he should demonstrate his performance capability in Service Group III for a significant period of time.*

He might then qualify for Service Group II, and should again demonstrate his capability for a significant period of time before being considered for unrestricted duties in Group I."

I think it is reasonable to suggest that three years is a "significant period of time."

I think it's time to start trying again.

12

Everything a Man Could Ask For

AFTER MY CRASH in 1962, the confidence I had in walking again was shared by my wife, Chris. When she's asked about it, she'll admit she had many apprehensions in those trying days; but she also shared with me a determination to continue a normal family life, and this required optimism and confidence on her part.

While I was still in the hospital, Chris and my mother took David and Debbie to the zoo, took them on picnics, and made every effort to keep things normal and routine. My crash and injuries were treated matter-of-factly. The children even sang, "Daddy 'jected from a Cougar and broke his legs," as they rode in the car to the hospital to visit me. That might seem somewhat unsympathetic, but David was three years old and Debbie was two, and they accepted the situation without any problems, fully believing Mommy's advice that Daddy was going to be just fine. Chris handled the whole situation exactly right; and her strength and common sense were major contributions to my steady recuperation, and to the children's understanding.

Both Chris and I believe in keeping our dealings with our fellow man straightforward and sincere. This enabled us to answer the children's questions about my accident and injuries with little difficulty. In particular I recall the first visit to the hospital that Chris and the children made after I was able to propel myself about in a wheelchair. David asked almost immediately, "Daddy, where are your feet?"

I replied, "Remember when Daddy's plane crashed? Well, Daddy got lots of 'hurts' then. One sharp piece of the crashed airplane cut this leg off right here, and this other leg was hurt so badly and got so sick from infection that the doctor had to cut it off very carefully—right here—so that Daddy's body wouldn't get too sick all over.

"But you just wait and see what happens! The doctor is going to have a man build Daddy some nice new legs—artificial ones made out of wood. They won't be as good as your legs, because God made yours; but they will be much better than no legs at all. In fact, Daddy will be able to walk again and to play with you in the swimming pool just like we used to do."

Self-consciousness has never been a part of my makeup—with or without legs. The family soon was accustomed to seeing me walking on my knees, unstrapping my legs, and "adjusting" myself to the needs of the moment. All of this was done with the same casualness another man might show in removing a pair of shoes.

This matter-of-factness has led to some amusing incidents. One I particularly remember was the time a writer was staying at our house overnight. I said "good night" to him at the door of the guest room, then ambled off to my own room, removing my legs before getting into bed. Suddenly I remembered something I wanted to tell our guest, so I knee-walked down the hall and knocked on his door. When he opened it, he stood there dumbfounded—momentarily stunned to see me more than a foot shorter than I had been when I'd said "good night" to him a few minutes before. He later told Chris that his feelings at that moment were the oddest he'd ever experienced.

Another amusing incident occurred after I had been ordered back to limited duty in the ferry squadron. I had also just been fitted with new prostheses that accommodated my pre-accident shoe size—8 wide. After sitting in the cockpits and manipulating the brake and rudder pedals of various aircraft, I became concerned about the lack of space between the top of the brake pedal and the underside of the instrument panel in some of the planes. Just one incident involving my toe getting caught on the underside of an instrument panel, would terminate my campaign to return to pilot status. The only solution was to reduce my foot size!

I went down to the Navy clothing store on the base, and asked the sailor on duty, "What is the smallest size military shoe you regularly stock?"

"Six medium, sir!" was his prompt reply.

"Good," I said. "I think I'll go to that size."

The sailor looked somewhat puzzled as he asked, "What size do you wear now?"

"Eight wide," I replied.

"Pardon me, sir, but I don't think you'll ever get them on," he remarked, now quite bewildered.

Realizing his concern now, but still failing to mention that I had two artificial legs I reassured him; "Oh, no, it's OK. I plan to reduce my foot size also!"

Returning to a normal life required the use of artificial legs that would enable me to function as normally as possible. Prosthetists have done many remarkable things, but there are some old notions and hard-to-change ideas even in this inventive field. For example, the general rule is to design "legs" that will best accommodate the wearer *while he has his shoes on.* The "legs" are not primarily designed for walking on "bare feet"; it is considered unlikely that an amputee would do much walking this way.

Before my accident I had been quite a watersports enthusiast. I liked to dive and water-ski and do many things that are usually done in bare feet. But wearing artificial legs and trying to steady myself on water-skis, negotiate wet ladders and keep my footing on a diving board soon sent me back to the prosthetists to suggest they design a pair of "legs" that would better accommodate me in "bare feet." If they could do this the "natural" way—the way God had designed natural legs—I could modify my shoes to fit.

This was a new idea—a double-amputee wanting to water-ski and dive and walk along beaches in his "bare feet." The prosthetists, though reluctant, set about changing the design of my "legs" to adjust to barefoot walking, balance and comfort. The end result was a better pair of "legs," "legs" that were far more natural. I had no problem with shoes. I'd buy a pair, lower the heels a bit, and be fitted perfectly. This change in limb design was another big step toward my resuming a normal life. I heartily endorse the practice of "barefoot" fitting and aligning for any active, below-the-knee amputee.

One of my many God-given attributes that contributed greatly to my recuperation is a good sense of balance. I experienced no difficulty in walking without the aid of crutches or even a cane the first time I tried walking on my new artificial legs. True, my gait was probably far from smooth, and it most certainly was quite uncomfortable; but it proved without a doubt that my balance was such that I would not have to depend on crutches or cane for assistance. I will always remember the joy that showed in the faces of Carl Thomsen and

Larry Jones as I took my first steps around their limb shop—unaided—on legs they had built for me with their own minds and hands.

It seems as though God gave me everything a man could ask for to enable me to bounce back from severe injury—confidence, determination, unbounded optimism, faith, and a strong, wonderful family. There is certainly little of my own doing in all of this, for I am what I have been made and what I have been given. Was it my mother who, during my childhood, made me a realist . . . who made it possible for me to accept later the loss of my natural legs and go on as before? Or was it a doctor, or friends, or Chris, or combinations of circumstances and experiences? Yes, probably all of these things were influencing factors, but the greatest motivating force was bigger than all of them. I have done nothing; God is the basic Source from whom every good attribute is derived that enables a man to do what people say I have done.

When I was in the hospital, I read the book *Jungle Pilot,* the story of Nate Saint, the missionary-pilot who was killed by the South American Indians he had tried to befriend. I was tremendously impressed by this story—so much so that I wrote to his wife, now Mrs. Abe Van Der Puy, to express my thanks for the meaning their lives have given mine. We continue to correspond with each other to this day.

When I finished the final chapter in Nate Saint's story, and reflected quietly on what this man had done, was that the moment in which I found renewed confidence, new faith, a new determination to struggle back toward normalcy? Had Nate Saint reached out, with God's help, and given me just that little extra spirit to guarantee my future progress?

When I gave a talk before a young people's group in Monterey—several years after the crash —a girl of about twelve asked me a searching question. She asked, "Were you as concerned about handicapped people before the accident as you are now?" After reflecting for a moment I replied, "No, in all honesty I was not." Before becoming an amputee, I was less aware of and less sympathetic to the problems of this group.

Today I'm taking every opportunity to promote a realization of the untapped potential of the so-called "handicapped." Is it because I have artificial legs? Or is it because of that little girl's question?

I honestly don't know. But I do know that whatever I've needed in my mental, physical, and emotional makeup has been provided—in different ways—by God.

In my profession—flying—I've also been given everything I could ask for. This includes enthusiasm, coordination, and the many, many factors which combine to produce a genuine love of flying and the ability to do a good job in the cockpit.

The sky is my realm, by nature and by choice. Nothing better illustrates the sheer joy I receive from flying than the experiences I had during my training days and as a flight instructor.

During advanced-training syllabus in the F9F-2 Panther jet fighter, another student and I were assigned a low-level reconnaissance hop. Among other checkpoints, the flight path followed a highway and a long stretch of railroad track. The object was to navigate—using landmarks only—and to pick out simulated enemy targets (trains, bridges, etc.), flying at as low an altitude as was permitted.

An instructor would be flying well above us to keep us out of trouble.

Off we went, and, true to my instructions, I flew the Panther as close to the ground as the instructor would allow, taking up the lead position and ticking off about 350 miles an hour.

When we reached the railroad tracks, I saw some men working on the rails. Some of them were standing on a flatcar. Although I passed over "the enemy" with many feet to spare, they weren't too convinced; and I still have the picture fresh in my mind of men diving to the left and right off that flatcar.

Too preoccupied with the "attack" to watch my flight path, I watched the chaos on the flatcars happily. Then I heard a fast shout in my earphones: *"Watch out for wires!"*

The wires were dead ahead and much too close to get over, so I did the only thing I could do—I flew under them, with about six feet to spare.

The instructor, observing all of this with responsible concern, was definitely relieved by the outcome; but he advised us to gain some altitude and refrain from making our "attacks" quite so realistic.

I believe that the men who are really captivated by the thrill of flying and who make the best pilots —at least fighter pilots—are those who give instructors gray hairs on occasion with shenanigans such as this.

My most dramatic demonstration of flying enthusiasm and ability—which almost ruined my career and gained me an official letter of reprimand—occurred when I was an instructor.

I had the opportunity to fly a T-28 to Mansfield, Ohio, just a few miles from my home in Oberlin, for the Fourth of July holiday. Filled with the spirit of the Fourth, the love of making an airplane perform to its maximum and pride at being a Navy fighter instructor, I proceeded to put on a low-lever air show near the edge of Oberlin, which is where my sister Connie lived. A T-28 performing aerobatics at low level makes a lot of noise, and there wasn't much doubt that many Oberlin residents witnessed the free show.

Pleased with my fine performance, I flew the airplane back to Mansfield, only to find out that I had been reported. A branch of the Federal Aeronautics Administration in Cleveland had telephoned airfields in the area, including Mansfield, asking if they had any knowledge of a Navy T-28, number such-and-such. I'd flown so low over Oberlin, somebody actually had been able to read the bureau number on the airplane. (I later received a photograph of the airplane, taken by a woman from her back porch as the plane skimmed over some nearby trees.)

Not so elated anymore, I quietly finished my Oberlin holiday by flying back to Whiting Field in Florida, where I was met by a duty officer.

"Hm-m-m," he smiled sarcastically. "Have a good time? I had a call from a fellow in Ohio about the altitude at which you like to fly."

I knew then and there I was in trouble. An investigation followed, and I was grounded for a few weeks. There was even the possibility that I could lose my wings; I never realized how much I truly loved flying until that threat loomed up on the horizon.

When I say I have everything a man could ask for, I mean as I am now, without natural legs. I can fly as well as I could before the crash. Whatever I've needed to compensate for the loss of my legs has been supplied by God, by family, by friends, doctors, and prosthetists.

I just may be the most fortunate man in the world.

13

The Late Frank Ellis

By ANY reasonable odds, I should have been killed in the crash that took my legs. From that moment on, I owed my life to God.

The Frank Ellis that *was* is no more. I've come to know the power of faith, the problems of the handicapped, their need for practical encouragement, and the larger, more general, and vital necessity of changing the outdated, entrenched public attitude toward the disabled.

It will come as no surprise that I have been asked to speak in churches, and before youth groups and civic and business associations; and I have spoken many times on behalf of organizations serving the handicapped.

I can say frankly that I don't much care for speaking and writing, or for putting myself on display, not even when awards are involved. I have a large, active family, and between my Naval duties and my continued efforts to get back the flying job I can do best, there is precious little time

I can enjoy with my wife and children or devote to a peaceful, productive home life.

Nevertheless, I am delighted to go anywhere, do anything reasonably possible, to take the case of the handicapped to the public. It is one of the great tragedies in our modern, supposedly sophisticated society that the loss of a leg or an arm often means automatic expulsion from the role of "useful human being."

I do not, in any sense, submit that all the handicapped should be treated alike. I do submit emphatically, however, that each man must be judged according to his individual merits and abilities. Any attitude ... any set of rules ... any generality of any kind that blocks this kind of objective judgment is not only wrong, it is patently unfit for an enlightened society.

"Hire the Handicapped" is a nice phrase, but it gives precisely the wrong impression—as if asking an employer to be charitable—and, furthermore, it is generally inappropriate. "Handicapped" is really an overworked, inaccurate word. A one-armed man who was a good accountant or engineer before his accident could be equally as good after his accident. He doesn't have any "handicap" at all in terms of his job—except in the eyes of a potential employer who can see only the empty sleeve.

Take a limb away from a man, and if he has

determination, he's likely to become *better* at his trade than he was before.

I've spent a good part of my life during the past five years in closer association with others who have lost a part of themselves somewhere along the way. These are the so-called "handicapped" . . . men, women, and children whose only objective in life is to return to normal living.

As of today, their hopes are dependent upon faith . . . faith in God, if they feel as I do, but also faith in their doctors, in friends, in our way of life, and, very importantly, in themselves.

Maybe this is why God's eucalyptus trees came up and grabbed me before I could smash into the ground and kill myself that day in 1962 . . . so I could say things like this to people like you . . . to all people . . . to a thirteen-year-old boy in Brooklyn, for example, who had both legs amputated after severe electrical injury. He wrote me:

> Thanks for all your advice. I bet I'll be
> able to walk all over the place as soon as
> they finish building my legs.

And he did, too. So much so that he rubbed some skin off his stumps and had to slow down for a few days.

He's young. Given time and good care, and continuing developments in the prosthetic field, he can grow up as normal as any man with natural legs.

At an annual dinner of the Goodwill Industries of Greater Detroit, a lady was pushed up to the speaker's platform in a wheel chair.

"God bless you, Son," she said to me. "This is what we've needed for so long."

God has indeed blessed me—not only because of all that has happened since the crash, but because He has given me a chance to talk to thirteen-year-olds in Brooklyn, ladies in wheel chairs and, just as important—to the "nonhandicapped". That is the great blessing . . . the lasting blessing . . . and although I have doubted many times that I could ever really be of help to other handicapped persons, or be any sort of inspiration to them, I clearly see God's hand in experiences like these.

It has been suggested (and probably prayed for by some people in the Navy) that I give up my flight career and devote my full time to administrative and public-relations work on behalf of the handicapped.

There are several things wrong with that theory. The first and foremost is that it would demonstrate just how really *hopeless* my case is. If I can't make it, and I'm their leader, so to speak, then who can?

It's not enough that I've come this far and been retained as a Group III pilot. There isn't any doubt in my mind (or the Navy's) that my proficiency deserves a higher group status. The only thing holding me back is their refusal to alter the viewpoint that a double-amputee simply *can't* be as proficient as another man. It simply won't do to have a double-amputee flying Naval aircraft alone and unaided. Besides, it sets a very bad precedent.

If I am to be of any significant value to the "handicapped," that value will come from the fact that I'm still fighting for acceptance. Publicity attends this effort, and as I progress as a pilot (as I am positive I will—in the Navy or out of it), even persons with unrelated problems will hear of my progress and be encouraged, as verified by the many cards and letters already received.

That's worth being saved for.

God paid special attention to me at a very critical few seconds in my life, and where He leads me I'll try to be man enough to follow. He has given me life, and I have complete faith that He will enable me to use it to the best of my ability and for His purpose.

In closing, I would like to stress two things. First, every single one of us is handicapped—physically, mentally, socially, and spiritually—to some degree; and although we seldom think about it, the person without faith has a far greater handicap than the person without feet.

Secondly, I have been given a tremendous amount of credit for what I have accomplished. This credit is due—but not to me. It is due God.

He has created me so that the transition from "walking" through life on God-given legs to taking that same walk on plastic legs has been quite automatic and relatively easy.

Surely NO MAN WALKS ALONE!